THE
BOOK OF IQ
TESTS

D0345738

33749

GORSEINON COLLEGE
LIBRARY

9 400/Lit
6.99

THE TIMES

BOOK OF IQ
TESTS

top uk puzzle editors

ken russell and philip carter

book 5

KOGAN
PAGE

London and Sterling, VA

Publisher's note
Every possible effort has been made to ensure that the information contained in this book is accurate at the time of going to press, and the publishers and authors cannot accept responsibility for any errors or omissions, however caused. No responsibility for loss or damage occasioned to any person acting, or refraining from action, as a result of the material in this publication can be accepted by the editor, the publisher or any of the authors.

First published in Great Britain and the United States in 2005 by Kogan Page Limited

Apart from any fair dealing for the purposes of research or private study, or criticism or review, as permitted under the Copyright, Designs and Patents Act 1988, this publication may only be reproduced, stored or transmitted, in any form or by any means, with the prior permission in writing of the publishers, or in the case of reprographic reproduction in accordance with the terms and licences issued by the CLA. Enquiries concerning reproduction outside these terms should be sent to the publishers at the undermentioned addresses:

120 Pentonville Road
London N1 9JN
United Kingdom
www.kogan-page.co.uk

22883 Quicksilver Drive
Sterling VA 20166–2012
USA

© Ken Russell and Philip Carter, 2005

The right of Ken Russell and Philip Carter to be identified as the authors of this work has been asserted by them in accordance with the Copyright, Designs and Patents Act 1988.

The views expressed in this book are those of the author, and are not necessarily the same as those of Times Newspapers Ltd.

British Library Cataloguing-in-Publication Data

A CIP record for this book is available from the British Library.

ISBN 0 7494 4391 X

Library of Congress Cataloging-in-Publication Data
Russell, Kenneth, A.
    The Times book of IQ tests. Book 5 / Ken Russell and Philip Carter. — 1st ed.
    p. cm.
Includes bibliographical references.
ISBN 0-7494-4391-X
1. Intelligence tests. 2. Self-evaluation. I. Carter, Philip J. II. Title.
BF431.3.R8725 2005
153.9'3—dc22   2005009402

Typeset by Saxon Graphics Ltd, Derby
Printed and bound in Great Britain by Clays Ltd, St Ives plc

Contents

Introduction

Of the different methods that purport to measure intelligence, the most famous is the IQ (Intelligence Quotient) test, which is a standardised test designed to measure human intelligence as distinct from attainments.

Intelligence quotient is an age-related measure of intelligence level. The word quotient means the result of dividing one quantity by another, and one definition of intelligence is mental ability or quickness of mind.

Usually, IQ tests consist of a graded series of tasks, each of which has been standardised with a large representative population of individuals in order to establish an average IQ of 100 for each test.

It is generally accepted that a person's mental ability develops at a constant rate until about the age of 13, after which development has been shown to slow down, and beyond the age of 18 little or no improvement is found.

When the IQ of a child is measured, the subject attempts an IQ test that has been standardised, with an average score recorded for each age group. Thus a 10-year-old child who scored the result that would be expected of a 12-year-old would have an IQ of 120, or 12/10 × 100:

$$\frac{\text{mental age (12)}}{\text{chronological age (10)}} \times 100 = 120 \, \text{IQ}$$

Because after the age of 18 little or no improvement is found, adults have to be judged on an IQ test whose average score is 100, and the results graded above and below this norm according to known test scores.

Like so many distributions found in nature, the distribution of IQ takes the form of a fairly regular bell curve (see Figure 0.1 below) in which the average score is 100 and similar proportions occur both above and below this norm.

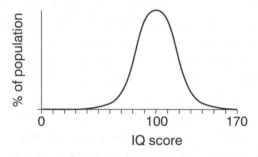

Figure 0.1   The bell curve

There are a number of different types of intelligence tests, for example Cattell, Stanford-Binet and Wechsler, and each have their own different scales of intelligence.

The Stanford-Binet is heavily weighted with questions involving verbal abilities and is widely used in the United States of America. The Weschler scales consist of two separate verbal and performance sub-scales each with its own IQ rating. On the Stanford-Binet scale half the population fall between 90 and 110 IQ, half of them above 100 and half of them below; 25 per cent score above 110; 11 per cent above 120; 3 per cent above 130 and 0.6 per cent above 140. At the other end of the scale the same kind of proportion occurs.

Although it is IQ tests that we are specifically concerned with in this book it should be pointed out that IQ tests are just one part of what is generally referred to as psychometric testing. Such test content may be addressed to almost any aspect of our intellectual or emotional make-up, including personality, attitude, intelligence or emotion. Psychometric tests are basically tools used for measuring the mind; the word metric means *measure* and the word psycho means *mind*. There are two types of psychometric tests that are usually used in tandem by employers. These are aptitude tests, which assess your abilities, and personality questionnaires, which assess your character and personality.

Aptitude tests are also known as cognitive, ability or intelligence (IQ) tests. Such tests are designed to test your ability to comprehend quickly under strictly timed conditions. Cognition may be broadly defined as knowing, perceiving and thinking and it is studied by psychologists because it reveals the extent of a person's ability to think.

There are many different types of tests. However, a typical test might consist of three sections each testing a different ability, usually comprising verbal reasoning, numerical ability and diagrammatic, or spatial, reasoning. In order to give you the opportunity to practise on all types of questions that you are likely to encounter in actual IQ tests, the tests that have been specially compiled for this book are multi-discipline and include a mix of verbal, numerical and diagrammatic questions, as well as additional questions involving logical thought processes as well as a degree of lateral thinking.

In the past 25 years psychometric testing has been brought into widespread use in industry because of the need for employers to ensure they place the right people in the right job at the outset. One of the main reasons for this is the high cost of errors in today's world of tight budgets and reduced profit margins. To recruit a new member of staff an employer has to advertise, consider each application, reduce the applicants to a shortlist, interview and then train the successful applicant. If the wrong hiring choice has been made, then the whole expensive process has to be repeated.

It is important that such tests are evaluated in tandem with each other as if a person scores well on an aptitude test it does not necessarily mean that they will be suited to the job, as whilst you may be good at doing something, you may dislike it intensely, and success in most tasks is heavily dependent on your personal qualities and your attitude.

Although it is generally accepted that a person's IQ remains constant throughout life, and, therefore, it is not possible to increase your actual IQ, it is possible to improve your performance on IQ tests by practising the many different types of question, and learning to recognise the recurring themes.

Besides their uses in improving one's performance on IQ tests, practice on the type of questions contained in this book has the added advantage of exercising the brain. Our brain needs exercise and care in the same way as other parts of the body. We eat the right foods to keep our heart healthy, we moisturise our skin to keep it from drying out and, just as gymnasts strive to increase their performance at whatever level they are competing by means of punishing training schedules and refinement of technique, there are exercises, or mental gymnastics, we can do to increase the performance of our brain and enhance quickness of thought.

Many people still have the outdated belief that there is little they can do to improve the brain they are born with and that brain cells continually degenerate with age: but, in fact, our brain cells continually develop new and stronger connections and adult brains can grow new cells irrespective of age.

The main thing is to use your brain continually. For example, the more we practise at tests of verbal aptitude the more we increase our ability to understand the meaning of words and use them effectively; the more we practise at maths the more confident we become when working with numbers, the better our ability to perform arithmetic operations accurately, and the quicker we become at performing these operations; and the more we practise our ability to move our fingers and manipulate small objects the more dextrous we become at operations involving this type of aptitude, and the quicker we become at performing them accurately.

The tests that follow have been newly compiled for this book and are not, therefore, standardised, so an actual IQ assessment cannot be given. However, a guide to assessing your performance for each test is provided below as well as a cumulative guide for your overall performance on all 10 tests.

A time limit of 90 minutes is allowed for each test. The correct answers are given at the end of the test, and you should award yourself one point for each completely correct answer. Calculators may be used to assist with solving numerical questions if preferred.

Use the following table to assess your performance:

One test:

Score	Rating
36–40	Exceptional
31–35	Excellent
25–30	Very good
19–24	Good
14–18	Average

Ten tests:

Score	Rating
351–400	Exceptional
301–350	Excellent
241–300	Very good
181–240	Good
140–180	Average

Test One: Questions

1.

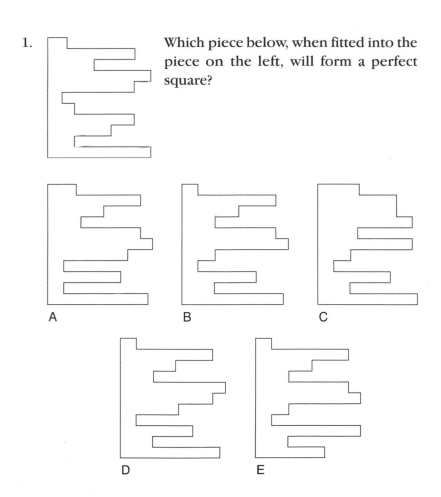

Which piece below, when fitted into the piece on the left, will form a perfect square?

A

B

C

D

E

2. Which word in brackets is most opposite to the word in capitals?

    PROSCRIBE (allow, stifle, promote, verify, indict)

3. 0, 1, 2, 4, 6, 9, 12, 16, ?

    What number should replace the question mark?

4. Which number is the odd one out?

    9678 4572 5261 5133 3527 6895 7768

5. Isotherm is to temperature as isobar is to: atmosphere, wind, pressure, latitude, current

6.

1	2	4	7
4	?	7	10
6	?	?	12
7	8	10	?

Which is the missing section?

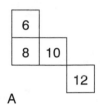

A

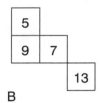

B

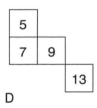

C

D

7. Which is the odd one out?

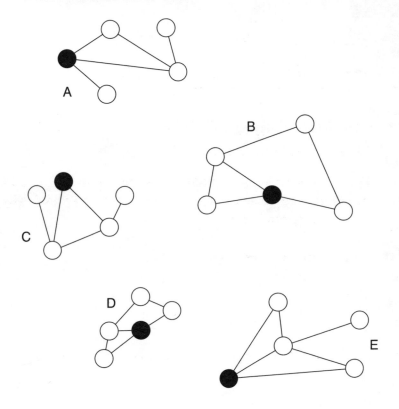

8. Identify two words (one from each set of brackets) that have a connection (analogy) with the words in capitals and relate to them in the same way.

    GRAM (energy, weight, scales)

    KNOT (water, rope, speed)

9.

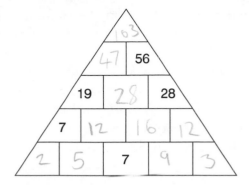

Each number in the pyramid is the sum of the two numbers immediately below it. Fill in the pyramid with the missing numbers.

10. Which is the odd one out?

A

B

C

D

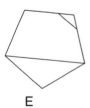

E

11. How many minutes is it before 12 noon, if 48 minutes ago it was twice as many minutes past 9 a.m.?

12. Complete the five words below in such a way that the two letters that end the first word also start the second word, and the two letters that end the second word also start the third word etc. The same two letters that end the fifth word also start the first word, to complete the cycle.

    ** IV **

    ** OT **

    ** IC **

    ** NG **

    ** RA **

13. Which is the odd one out?

    heptagon, triangle, hexagon, cube, pentagon

14. Switch A turns lights 1 and 2 on/off or off/on

   Switch B turns lights 2 and 4 on/off or off/on

   Switch C turns lights 1 and 3 on/off or off/on

   ◯ = ON

   ⬤ = OFF

   Switches C, A and B are thrown in turn with the result that
   Figure 1 turns into Figure 2. Which switch does not work
   at all?

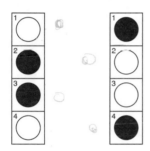

   Figure 1   Figure 2

15.

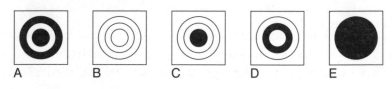

Which is the missing tile?

A   B   C   D   E

16. Which word in brackets is closest in meaning to the word in capitals?

BRUNT (dull, edifice, impact, tawny, nonsense)

17. Which of the following is not an anagram of a type of food?

PAST EIGHT

I CAN ROAM

WIN BOAR

CAN PEAK

COOL CHEAT

18.

What number should replace the question mark?

19.

N	O	I	
A	R	O	S
L		F	E

Work from square to adjacent square horizontally or vertically (but not diagonally) to spell out a 12-letter word. You must find the starting point, and provide the missing letters.

20. How many lines appear below?

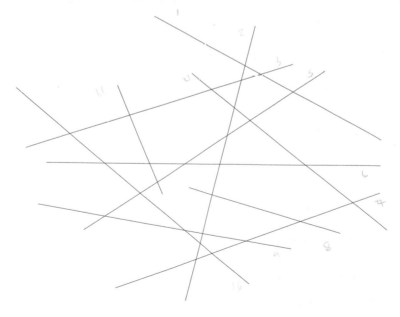

21.

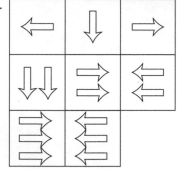

Which is the missing tile?

A

B

C

D

E

F

22. $6^7/_8$, $2^9/_{16}$, $5^5/_8$, $3^{13}/_{16}$, $4^3/_8$, ?

What number should replace the question mark?

23.

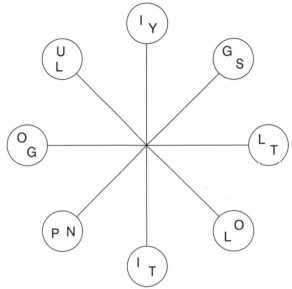

Work clockwise round the circles to spell out two eight-letter words that are synonyms. Each word commences in a different circle, and you must find the starting point of each. Every letter is used once each and all letters are consecutive.

24. 10, 30, 32, 96, 98, 294, 296, ?, ?

What two numbers should replace the question marks?

25. able, rot, son, king

Which word below shares a common feature with all the words above?

line, sit, take, hope, night

26. Identify two words (one from each set of brackets) that have a connection (analogy) with the words in capitals and relate to them in the same way.

    SEA (wet, swimmer, ship)

    SNOW (mountain, ice, skier)

27. Which word meaning LOCALITY becomes a word meaning TEMPO when a letter is removed?

28. Alf has four times as many as Jim, and Jim has three times as many as Sid. Altogether they have 192. How many has each?

29. Which is the only one of the following that is not an anagram of a word meaning *out of this world*?

    flow under

    sexed Utah

    enviable blue

    icier blend

30. A man has 53 socks in his drawer: 21 identical blue, 15 identical black and 17 identical red. The lights are fused and he is completely in the dark. How many socks must he take out to make 100 per cent certain he has a pair of black socks?

31.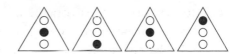

Draw the missing figure in the above sequence.

32. How many minutes is it before 12 noon if nine minutes ago it was twice as many minutes past 10 a.m.?

33. Which two words are closest in meaning?

conclave, medley, theme, conglomeration, dissertation, augury

34. broke rage prose cute dared   ?

Which word is missing?

palm hymn evil snow take

35. Find *five* consecutive numbers below that total 22.

7 3 9 6 4 1 3 7 9 3 5 4 1 7 6 5

36.

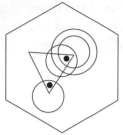

To which hexagon below can a dot be added so that both dots then meet the same conditions as the two dots in the hexagon above?

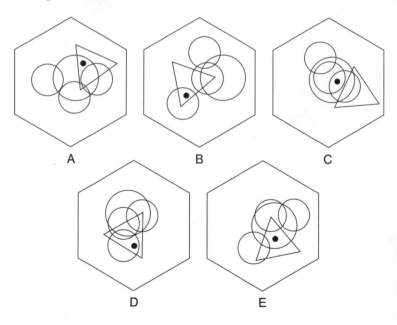

37. Find two words (4, 6) in this diagram. Letters are traced across the circle by chords. If the next letter is four letters or less away it will be found by tracing around the circumference. Clue: free flight.

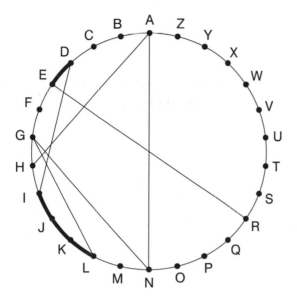

38.

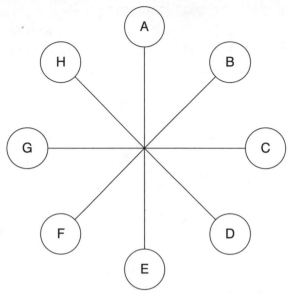

What letter is directly opposite the letter that is two letters away clockwise from the letter that is directly opposite the letter E?

39.

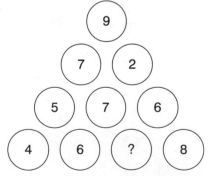

What number should replace the question mark?

40.

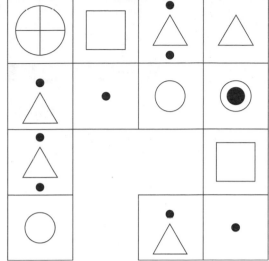

Which is the missing section?

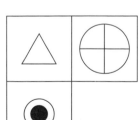

A

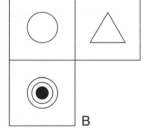

B

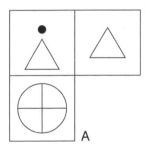

C

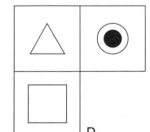

D

Test One: Answers

1. B

    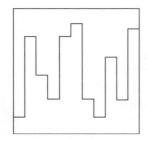

2. allow

3. 20: add 1, 1, 2, 2, 3, 3, 4, 4

4. 3527: in the others the sum of the first two numbers is equal to the sum of the second two numbers, for example 5+2 = 6+1

5. pressure

6. D: lines across proceed +1, +2, +3. Lines down proceed +3, +2, +1.

7. C: in all the others the black circle is connected to three white circles. In C it is only connected to two white circles.

8. weight, speed

9.

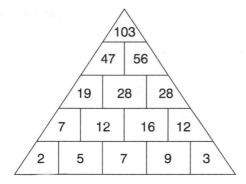

10. B: the rest are the same figure rotated

11. 44 minutes

    12 noon less 44 minutes = 11.16
    11.16 less 48 minutes = 10.28
    9 a.m. plus 88 minutes (44 × 2) = 10.28

12. SHIVER, EROTIC, ICICLE, LENGTH, THRASH

13. cube: it is a three-dimensional figure. The rest are all two-dimensional figures.

14. Switch A is faulty.

15. B: in each line and column, each of the three rings is shaded black once

16. impact

17. WIN BOAR = rainbow. The foods are spaghetti (PAST EIGHT), macaroni (I CAN ROAM), pancake (CAN PEAK) and chocolate (COOL CHEAT).

18. 4: looking across at the three circles, the number in the middle is the product of the two numbers in the same segment in the other two circles. Thus, $3 \times 2 = 6$, $7 \times 3 = 21$ and $4 \times 4 = 16$.

19. PROFESSIONAL

20. 11

21. D: in each line across and down the arrows point in each of three directions left, right and down. The number of arrows increases 1, 2, 3 in each row.

22. $5\frac{1}{16}$: there are two alternate sequences: $-1\frac{1}{4}$ and $+1\frac{1}{4}$

23. linguist, polyglot

24. 888, 890: the sequence progresses $\times 3$, $+2$

25. take: all words can be prefixed with PAR to form another word – parable, parrot, parson, parking, partake

26. swimmer, skier

27. place/pace

28. Alf 144, Jim 36, Sid 12

29. sexed Utah = exhausted. The words meaning out of this world are: wonderful (flow under), unbelievable (enviable blue), incredible (icier blend).

30. 40 socks. If he takes out 38 socks, although it is very unlikely, it is possible they could all be blue and red. To make 100 per cent certain that he also has a pair of black socks he must take out a further two socks.

31.

The black dot is moving up (then down) by one position at each stage.

32. 37 minutes: 12 noon less 37 minutes = 11.23. 11.23 less nine minutes = 11.14. 10 a.m. plus 74 minutes (2 × 37) = 11.14.

33. medley, conglomeration

34. evil: when joined together each pair of words forms another word – brokerage, prosecute, daredevil

35. 93541

36. D: so that one dot appears in the triangle and one circle; and the other dot appears in the triangle and three circles

37. HANG GLIDER

38. G

39. 0: looking at lines of numbers from the top: $9 \times 8 = 72$; $72 \times 8 = 576$; $576 \times 8 = 4608$

40. C: each opposite corner block of four squares are identical

Test Two: Questions

1.

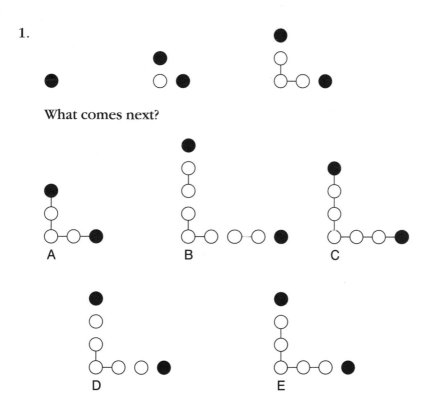

What comes next?

2. Which four-letter word, when placed in the brackets, will complete a word on the left and start another word on the right?

   RAM (****) RIDGE

3.

20	22	19	21
17	19	16	?
19	21	?	20
16	18	15	?

Which is the missing section?

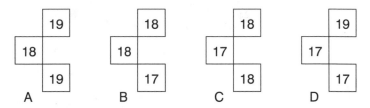

A   B   C   D

4. ligno- is to wood as vitro- is to wool, glass, stone, water, paper?

5.

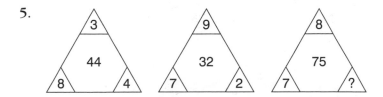

What number should replace the question mark?

6. Solve the anagrams to find a well-known saying. The number of letters in each word is shown.

   (**** ** ********)(**** *******)

   (asserting craft)(hint of antic)

7.

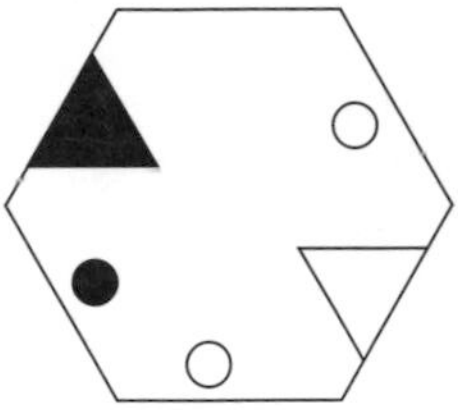

is to:

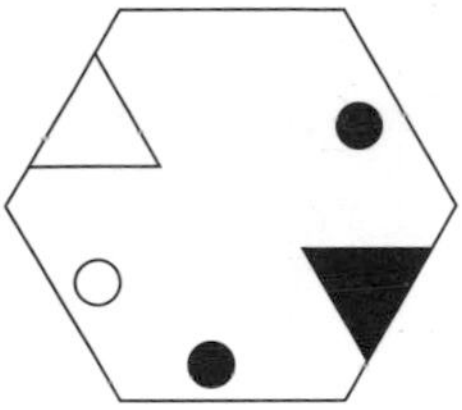

as

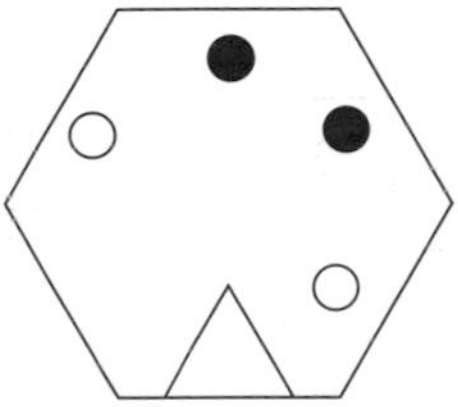

is to:

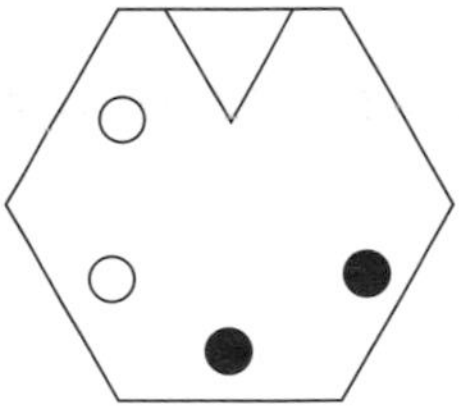

A 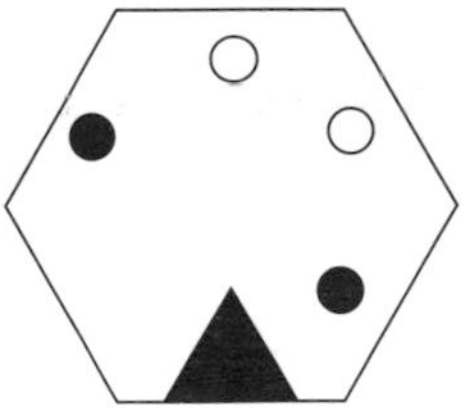   B 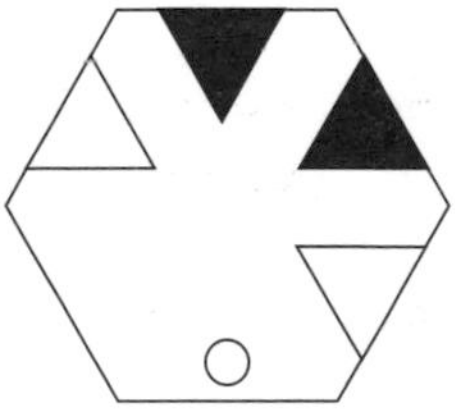   C

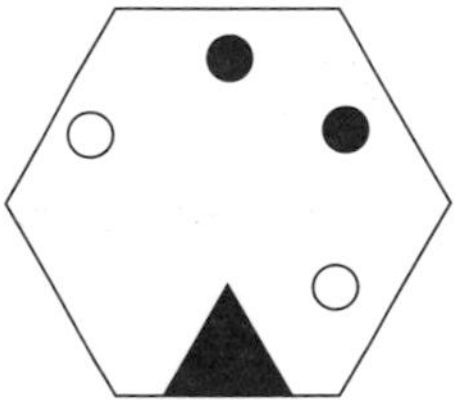

D 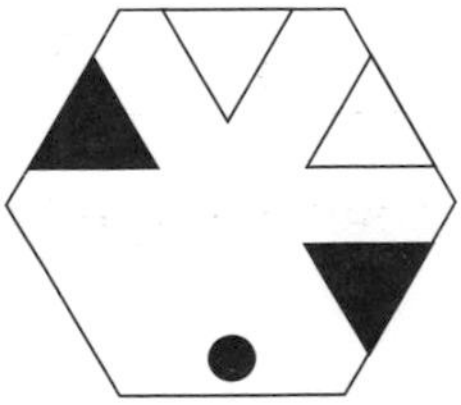   E

8. 0, 4 ,2, 6, 3, 7, 3.5, ?

    What number should replace the question mark?

9. Identify two words (one from each set of brackets) that have a connection (analogy) with the words in capitals and relate to them in the same way

    LONGITUDE (degree, tropics, meridian)

    LATITUDE (parallel, line, equinox)

10.

5	2	3	10
6	4	1	11
1	9	?	12
12	?	6	?

Which is the missing section?

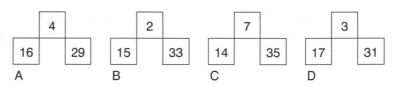

A   B   C   D

11. Which word in brackets is closest in meaning to the word in capitals?

    MONITOR (observe, order, meddle, intrude, conclude)

12.

Looking at lines across and down, if the first two tiles are combined to produce the third tile, with the exception that like symbols are cancelled out, which of the above tiles is incorrect, and with which of the tiles below should it be replaced?

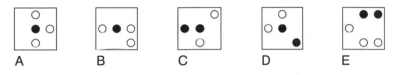

A   B   C   D   E

13. Which two words are most opposite in meaning?

liberty, frivolity, chastity, sobriety, irrationality, polarity

14.

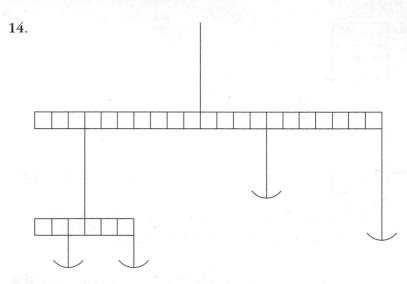

Insert four weights of 2 units, 3 units, 4 units and 6 units respectively so that the scales balance perfectly.

15. The following clue leads to which pair of rhyming words?

measure bulk of grass fodder

16.

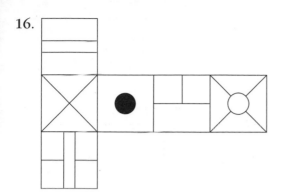

When the above is folded to form a cube, which is the only one of the following that *can* be produced?

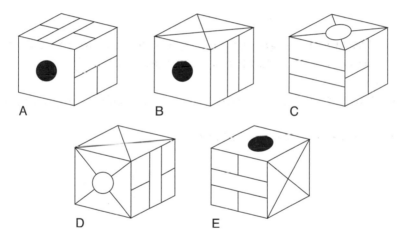

A   B   C

D   E

17. Which is the odd one out?

femur, mandible, fibula, tibia, patella

18. My watch was correct at noon, after which it started to lose 17 minutes per hour until six hours ago it stopped completely. It now shows the time as 2.52 p.m. What time is it now?

19.

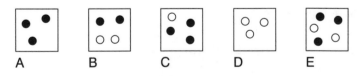

Insert all the letters of the phrase UNSPOILT LOCAL into the remaining blank spaces once each only, to produce two words that form a phrase. Clue: things are not always what they appear.

20.

Which is the missing tile?

A   B   C   D   E

21.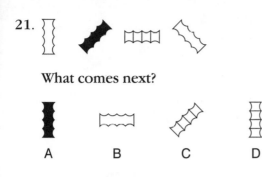

What comes next?

A   B   C   D   E

F   G   H

22. dopiness, uncloaking, dishwasher

Which word below has a feature in common with all the words above?

gallant, crossfire, whirlwind, assault

23. 1, 101, 15, 4, 29, –93, 43, –190, ?

What number should replace the question mark?

24.

A	B	C	D	E	
F	G	H	I	J	
K	L	M	N	O	
P	Q	R	S	T	
U	V	W	X	Y	Z

What letter is two letters above the letter two letters to the left of the letter immediately above the letter three letters to the right of the letter Q?

25. 15, 5, 8, 24, 21, 7, 10, 30, ?, ?, ?, 36, 33

What three numbers are missing?

26.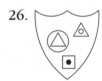

Which shield below has most in common with the shield above?

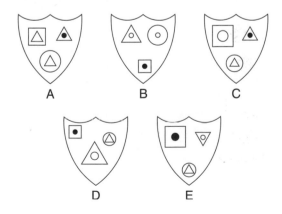

27. Using the four letters below only, create a seven-letter word.

   UMNI

28.

5	
8	5
1	7

4	
7	6
1	9

?	
9	1
1	3

   What number should replace the question mark?

29. Switch A turns lights 1 and 2 on/off or off/on
   Switch B turns lights 2 and 4 on/off or off/on
   Switch C turns lights 1 and 3 on/off or off/on
   Switch D turns lights 3 and 4 on/off or off/on

    = ON

   ○ = OFF

   Switches D, C, A and B are thrown in turn with the result that Figure 1 turns into Figure 2. Which switch does not work at all?

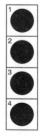 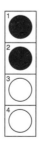

Figure 1   Figure 2

30. Which word in brackets is closest in meaning to the word in capitals?

   FUSE (muzzle, explode, coalesce, immobilise, tighten)

31.

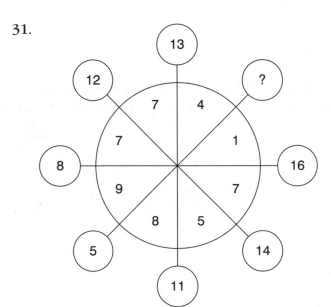

   What number should replace the question mark?

32.

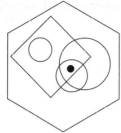

To which hexagon below can a dot be added so that it then meets the same conditions as in the hexagon above?

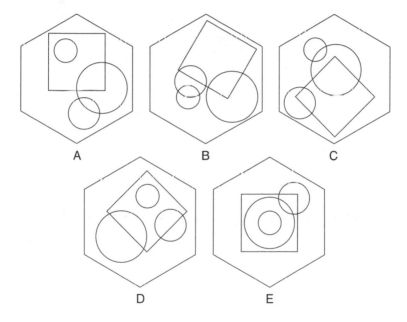

A   B   C

D   E

33. You have 59 cubic blocks. What is the minimum number that needs to be taken away in order to construct a solid cube with none left over?

34. What word meaning DEDUCE becomes a word meaning PROPEL when a letter is removed?

35.

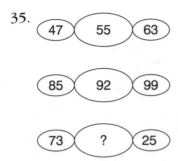

What number should replace the question mark?

36. What is the longest word in the English language that can be produced out of the set of letters below? Letters may only be used once in the word so produced.

FEUMOPXCTW

37.

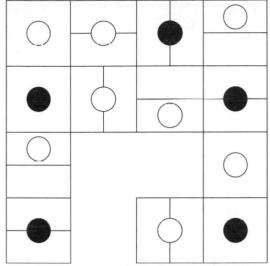

Which is the missing section?

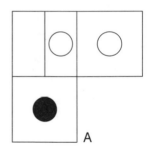

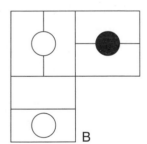

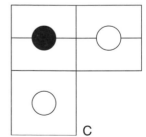

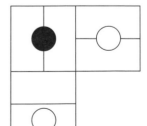

A

B

C

D

38.

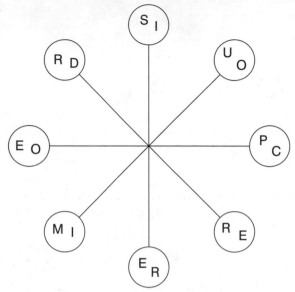

Work clockwise round the circles to spell out two eight-letter words that are antonyms. Each word commences in a different circle, and you must find the starting point of each. Every letter is used once each and all letters are consecutive.

39.

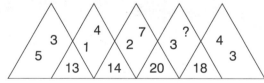

What number should replace the question mark?

40.

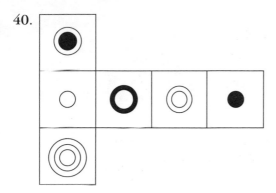

When the above is folded to form a cube, which is the only one of the following that *can* be produced?

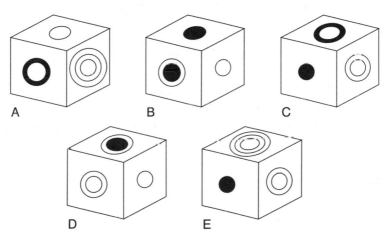

Test Two: Answers

1. E: the number of white dots is increased by one each time, both vertically and horizontally, and all white dots are connected

2. PART: RAMPART and PARTRIDGE

3. B: lines across proceed +2, –3, +2. Lines down proceed –3, +2, –3.

4. glass

5. 5: $(8 + 7) \times 5 = 75$

6. fact is stranger than fiction

7. B: black objects turn to white and vice versa

8. 7. 5: the sequence proceeds +4, ÷2, +4, etc

9. meridian, parallel

10. B: in lines and columns, add the first three numbers to arrive at the fourth number

11. observe

12.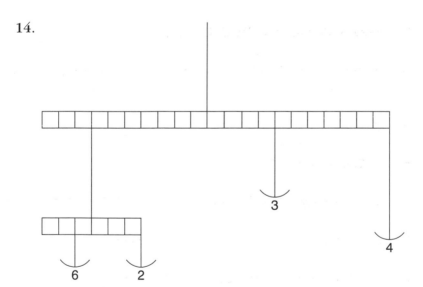

Tile 7 is incorrect, and should be replaced by tile B.

13. frivolity, sobriety

14.

$6 \times 1 = 2 \times 3: 7 \times 8 \, (6 + 2) = 56$

$11 \times 4 = 44$
$4 \times 3 = 12$
$44 + 12 = 56$

15. weigh hay

16. D

17. mandible: it is the jaw bone, the rest are bones in the leg

18. 10 p.m.

> 12 noon = 12 noon
> 1 p.m. = 12.43
> 2 p.m. = 1.26
> 3 p.m. = 2.09
> 4 p.m. = 2.52
> +6 hours = 10 p.m.

19. OPTICAL ILLUSION

20. A: each line across and down contains five black dots and four white dots

21. A: the figure is tumbling 45° at each stage and alternates white/black/striped

22. crossfire: all words contain an embedded tree – do(pine)ss, uncl(oak)ing, dishw(ash)er, cross(fir)e

23 57: there are two alternate sequences: +14, –97

24. C

25. 27, 9, 12: the sequence progresses ÷3, +3, ×3, –3 repeated

26. D: it contains a triangle in a circle, a circle in a triangle (with the same orientation of the triangle) and a black dot in a square

27. minimum

28. 7: 91 ÷ 13

29. Switch D is faulty.

30. coalesce

31. 17: it is the sum of the two digits (9 + 8) in the quadrant directly opposite

32. E: so that the dot appears in two circles and the square

33. 32: the next cube number below 64 (4 × 4 × 4) is 27 (3 × 3 × 3). In order to construct a solid cube, therefore, with none left over, 59 – 27 = 32 blocks need to be taken away.

34. DERIVE/DRIVE

35. 49: (73 + 25) ÷ 2

36. COMPUTE

37. D: the last two rows of figures repeat the first two rows of figures in reverse

38. MEDIOCRE, SUPERIOR

39. 8: each number in the segment at the bottom is the sum of the four numbers in the sections either side. Thus: 8 + 3 + 4 + 3 = 18

40. E

Test Three: Questions

1.

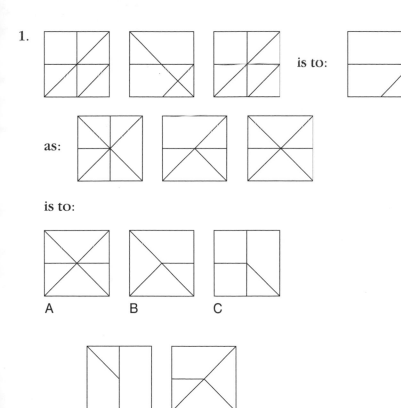

is to:

as:

is to:

A   B   C

D   E

2. Which is the odd one out?

    cymbal, marimba, vibraphone, trombone, glockenspiel

3. stationary, less, stationery, principal, fewer, principle

    Place the words above alongside their correct definition below:

    head of school
    fundamental truth
    standing still
    writing materials
    smaller in amount
    smaller in number

4. Which is the odd number out?

    462 683 385 198 253 781 594

5. PURE AS TUFT is an anagram of which two words that are opposite in meaning?

6.

A	B	C	D	E	
F	G	H	I	J	
K	L	M	N	O	
P	Q	R	S	T	
U	V	W	X	Y	Z

Which letter is midway between the letter two letters below the letter immediately to the left of the letter G, and the letter three letters above the letter immediately to the right of the letter V?

7. 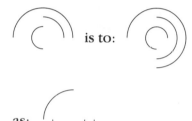 is to:

as:

is to:

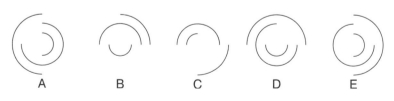

   A   B   C   D   E

8.

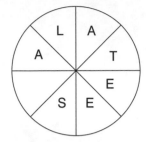 

Complete two eight-letter words, one in each circle, and both reading clockwise. The words are synonyms. You must find the starting points and provide the missing letters.

9.   1, 50, 6, 45, 11, 40, 16, 35, 21, ?, ?

Which numbers should replace the question marks?

10. Arrange the words below into alphabetical order:

acescence, acetamide, acerbated, acetified, acellular, acescency, acetabula, acerbates

11.

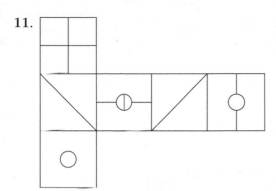

When the above is folded to form a cube, which is the only one of the following that *can* be produced?

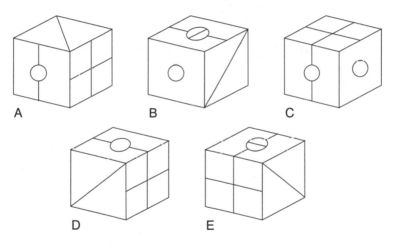

A B C

D E

12.

3	9	1	2	8	3
9	?	?	2	1	9
1	?	?	3	9	1
2	1	9	3	8	2
8	3	9	1	2	8
3	8	2	1	9	3

Which is the missing section?

8	3
8	2

A

3	8
2	8

B

8	2
8	3

C

2	8
3	8

D

13. Solve the anagram in brackets to correctly complete the quotation with a 10-letter word.

'The difference between golf and (torn veg men) is that in golf you cannot improve your lie' *George Deukmejian*

14.

Which shield should replace the question mark?

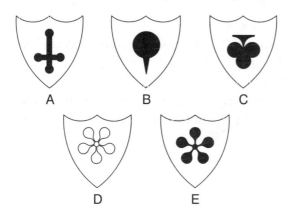

15.

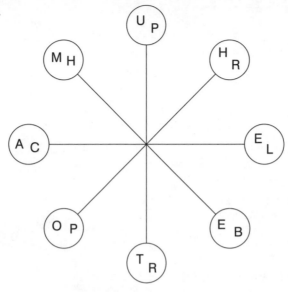

Take one letter from each circle in turn and using each letter once only find two eight-letter words that are similar in meaning. Both words read clockwise and each starts in a different circle.

16. What letters should replace the question marks?

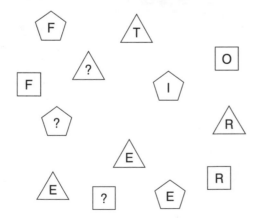

17.

What number should replace the question mark?

18. bizarre is to outlandish as eccentric is to: eerie, quirky, esoteric, weird, curious

19. On taking delivery of a consignment of eggs the market stall owner was furious to find that several were cracked. In fact, on counting them up in order to assess the damage he found that 72 were cracked, which was 12 per cent of the total consignment. How many eggs in total were in the consignment?

20.
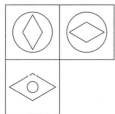

Which is the missing tile?

A   B   C   D   E

21. MTD is to PXB as FRJ is to?

22. A B C D E F G H

What letter is two letters to the left of the letter immediately to the right of the letter three letters to the right of the letter A?

23.

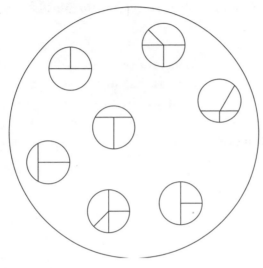

Which circle below should be placed in the large circle above?

A   B   C   D   E

24. Using the five letters below only, create a nine-letter word.

    LOPER

25. 16, 23, 19, 19, 22, 15, 25, ?

    What number should replace the question mark?

26. Simplify:

    $$\frac{14}{55} \div \frac{56}{77}$$

    as the lowest fraction.

27.

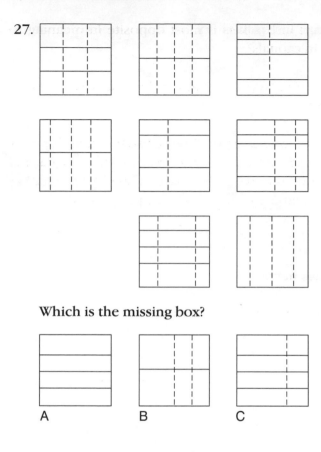

Which is the missing box?

28. Which word in brackets is most opposite in meaning to the word in capitals?

    PLAUSIBLE (appropriate, improbable, clichéd, artificial, distasteful)

29. The cost of an identical three-course lunch for four people was £56.00. The main course cost twice as much as the sweet and the sweet cost twice as much as the starter. How much did the main course cost per person?

30. aplomb, dodge, graph, jerk, ?

    What comes next?

    laugh, maroon, link, nickel, midnight

31.

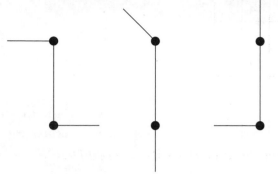

What comes next?

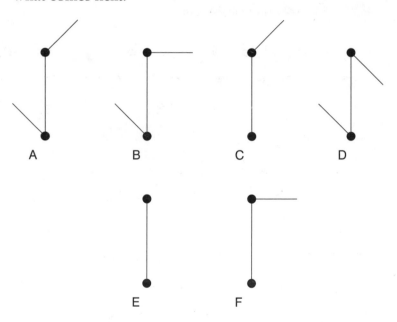

32.

			14	
	22			
			34	
41				
		53		?

What number should replace the question mark?

33. OVATE GNOME is an anagram of which familiar phrase (3, 1, 4, 2)? Clue: make haste.

34.

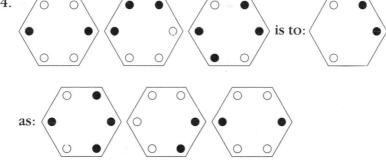

is to:

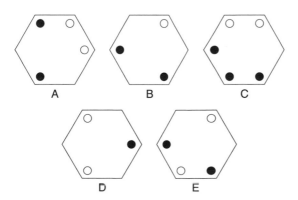

is to:

A   B   C

D   E

35.

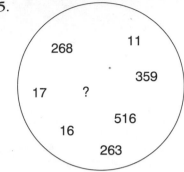

What number should replace the question mark?

36.

R	I	N		
T	O	G		
N	S	A	S	D
		A	T	E
		T	C	H

Find the starting point and work from letter to adjacent letter vertically, horizontally and diagonally to spell out a 17-letter phrase (2, 7, 8).

37.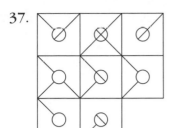

Which is the missing tile?

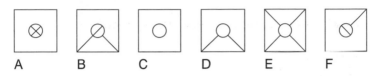

A   B   C   D   E   F

38.

At each stage the black dot moves three corners clockwise and the white dot moves four corners anti-clockwise. After how many stages will both dots be together in the same corner?

39. A A S G P A H A M

R S E E I I U G A

* * * * * * * * *

The name of which reptile can be placed on the bottom row to complete nine three-letter words reading downwards?

40.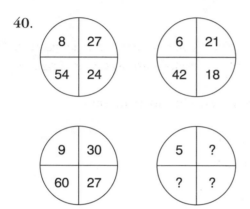

What numbers should replace the question marks?

Test Three: Answers

1. E: only lines that appear three times in the same position in the first three squares are carried forward to the final square

2. trombone: the rest are percussion instruments

3. head of school = principal
   fundamental truth = principle
   standing still = stationary
   writing materials = stationery
   smaller in amount = less
   smaller in number = fewer
   (score 1 point if all answers are correct)

4. 683: in the other numbers add the first and last digits to arrive at the middle digit

5. PAST, FUTURE

6. L

7. D: to each arc, add a quarter of a circle clockwise

8. ESCALATE, HEIGHTEN

9. 30, 26: there are two alternate sequences. Add 5 starting at 1. Subtract 5 starting at 50.

10. acellular, acerbated, acerbates, acescence, acescency, acetabula, acetamide, acetified

11. D

12. B: start at the bottom left-hand corner square and work along the bottom row, then back along the next row up etc, repeating the numbers 38219

13. government

14. E: each line across and down contains one each of the three symbols. In each line one symbol is black, and one is upside down.

15. PAMPHLET, BROCHURE

16. VHU: the numbers spelled out below are the number of sides in the figures in which they appear

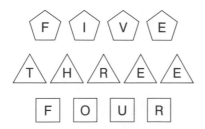

17. 4: 6 × 9 = 54 (reading down the middle two blocks)

18. quirky

19. 600: $72 \div 12 \times 100$

20. C: looking across and down the triangles turn through 90°

21. IVH: the first letter moves three places in the alphabet forwards: FghI; the second letter moves four letters in the alphabet forwards: RstuV; the third letter moves two places in the alphabet backwards: JiH

22. C

23. C: each circle is repeated rotated

24. PROPELLER

25. 11: there are two alternate sequences: +3 and −4

26. $\dfrac{14}{55} \times \dfrac{77}{56} = \dfrac{1}{5} \times \dfrac{7}{4} = \dfrac{7}{20}$

27. C: each row and column contains six complete lines and six broken lines

28. improbable

29. £8.00 per person:

    starter = 1 unit
    sweet = 2 units
    main course = 4 units
    = 7 units in total

    Therefore, cost per unit = £56 ÷ 7 = £8.00.
    The main course, therefore, cost 4 × 8 = 32 (or £8.00 per person).

30. maroon: the letters start and finish with the alphabetic sequence: ABcDEfGHiJKlMN

31. C: the top arm moves 45° clockwise at each stage and the bottom arm moves 90° clockwise

32. 55: each number indicates its position in the grid. 55 indicates row 5 column 5.

33. GET A MOVE ON

34. B: only dots that appear in the same position just twice in the first three hexagons are carried forward to the final hexagons

35. 12: add the digits of each three-figure number to obtain the two-digit numbers

36. NO STRINGS ATTACHED

37. C: in each row and column only lines that are common to the first two squares are carried forward to the final square

38. They will never appear together in the same corner as in a heptagon three corners clockwise is the same as four corners anti-clockwise.

39. CHAMELEON: to produce ARC, ASH, SEA, GEM, PIE, AIL, HUE, AGO, MAN

40.

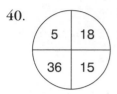

Top left is a third of bottom right, bottom right is three less than top right and top right is half of bottom left.

Test Four: Questions

1.

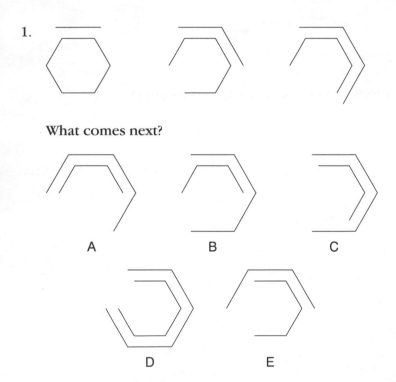

What comes next?

A   B   C

D   E

2.   100, 97.4, 94.8, ? , 89.6, 87

What number should replace the question mark?

3.

E	A	D
		I
P	A	

Start at one of the four corner letters and spiral clockwise round the perimeter, finishing at the centre letter to spell out a nine-letter word. You must provide the missing letters.

4. Which number is the odd one out?

   9654 4832 5945 7642 7963 8216 3649

5. Which two words are closest in meaning?

   qualified, practicable, puissant, feasible, mundane, fine

6. Identify two words (one from each set of brackets) that have a connection (analogy) with the words in capitals and relate to them in the same way.

   FIRST (second, next, last)

   PENULTIMATE (last, third, previous)

7. Find five consecutive numbers below that total 23.

   6 2 9 3 4 7 2 9 3 2 6 4 9 1 2

8.

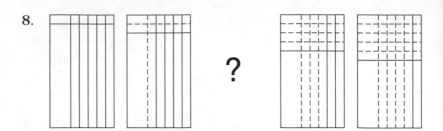

Draw the missing figure in the above sequence.

9. Which word in brackets is most opposite to the word in capitals?

    SLEEK (sordid, unimaginative, disorderly, dishevelled, oblique)

10.

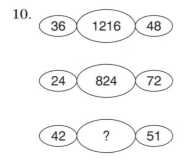

What number should replace the question mark?

11. Change one letter only in each of the words below to produce a familiar phrase.

    AND FEEL SO TIE WIRE

12. Which is the odd one out?

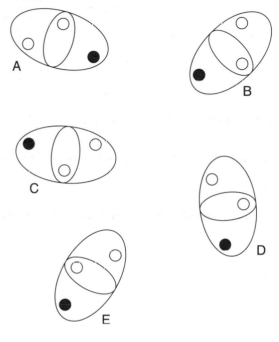

13. Which is the odd one out?

   trivet, tributary, triptych, trident, triad

14.

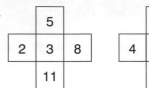

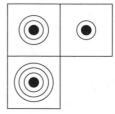

What number should replace the question mark?

15. 5862 is to 714
   and 3498 is to 1113
   and 9516 is to 156
   therefore 8257 is to ?

16.

Which is the missing tile?

A   B   C   D   E   F

17. mohair is to wool as shantung is to: silk, cotton, linen, nylon, fabric

18.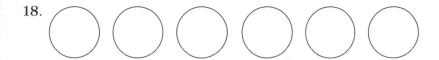

   Place the numbers 1–6 into the circles, one number per circle, so that: the sum of the numbers 4 and 1, and all the numbers between them total 12; the sum of the numbers 4 and 6, and all the numbers between them total 21; the sum of the numbers 2 and 1, and all the numbers between them total 8.

19. If meat in a river (3 in 6) is T(HAM)ES, can you find a monkey in a tall building (3 in 10)?

20.

   What comes next in the above sequence?

A   B   C   D   E

21.

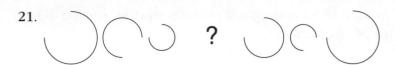

Which arc is missing?

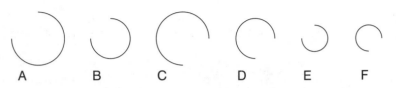

A   B   C   D   E   F

22. Which four bits can be joined together to form two words that have opposite meanings?

ERT, UCE, DES, END, EXP, EAR, AND, SIP, RED, GOS

23.

7	10	13	16
9	12	?	18
11	?	?	20
13	16	19	22

Which is the missing section?

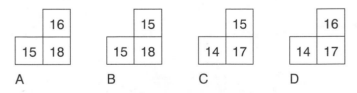

A   B   C   D

24. Identify two words that sound alike but are spelled differently, which mean:

    a straight line connecting two points on a curve

    rope

25. Find the ages of Mary, George, Alice, Claire and Stephen if:

    Mary + George = 33 years between them
    Alice + Claire = 95 years between them
    Stephen + Mary = 72 years between them
    Mary + Claire = 87 years between them
    Stephen + George = 73 years between them

26.

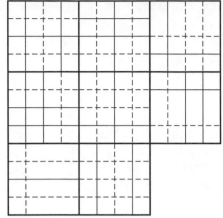

Which is the missing tile?

A   B   C

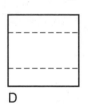

D   E

27. Using the four letters below only, create a seven-letter word.

CILT

28. 53 (3) 59
92 (4) 98
34 (2) 38
71 (?) 79

What number should replace the question mark?

29.

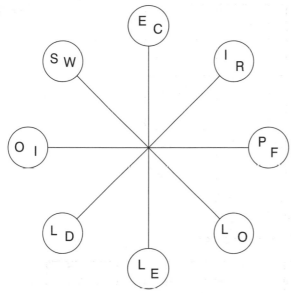

Work clockwise round the circles to spell out two eight-letter words that are synonyms. Each word commences in a different circle, and you must find the starting point of each. Every letter is used once each and all letters are consecutive.

30.   **?**

Draw the missing figure in the above sequence.

31. abashed, derail, little, ?

What comes next?

mellow, entail, leader, elicit, status

32. Produce an eight-letter word by joining together two of these four-letter sets.

    cred, agon, lues, once, deva, some, come, pent

33.

20	14	12	24	33
3	10	16	15	18
17	7	4	8	6
5	1	9	30	36
39	21	13	2	11

What number is three places away from itself plus three, two places away from itself multiplied by two, two places away from itself less four and two places away from itself divided by three?

34.   **?**

What comes next?

A   B   C   D   E

35.

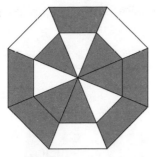

What percentage of the figure is shaded?

36.

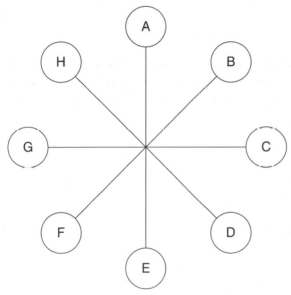

What letter is two letters away clockwise from the letter that is directly opposite the letter three letters away anti-clockwise from the letter C?

37.

B	E	R
I	E	
	T	A

Spiral clockwise round the perimeter and finish at the centre square to spell out a nine-letter word. You must find the starting point and provide the missing letters.

38. What is one-third of one-quarter of one-fifth of one-half of 120?

39.

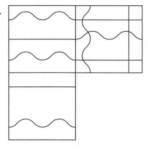

Which is the missing tile?

A

B

C

D

E

40.

1	10	7	16
28	19	22	13
25	34	31	40
?	43	46	37

What number should replace the question mark?

Test Four: Answers

1. B: the inner hexagon is being dismantled one side at a time working anti-clockwise, while the outer hexagon is being constructed one side at a time working clockwise

2. 92.2: deduct 2.6 at each stage

3. DISAPPEAR

4. 3649: in all the others multiply the first two digits together to produce the number formed by the last two digits

5. practicable, feasible

6. second, last

7. 72932

8.

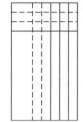

Vertical lines turn dotted, one at a time at each stage. One horizontal line is added at each stage, and the previous lines become dotted.

9. dishevelled

10. 1417: $42 ÷ 3 = 14, 51 ÷ 3 = 17$

11. ADD FUEL TO THE FIRE

12. E: the rest are the same figure rotated

13. tributary: in the other words the prefix tri- refers to three

14. 7: the numbers round the centre increase by seven (in the others they increase by three and five respectively)

15. 157: $7 + 8 = 15, 2 + 5 = 7$

16. B: looking across an outer circle is removed, looking down an outer circle is added

17. silk

18. 425136 or 631524

19. SKYSCR(APE)R

20. D: looking across, the dot in the top left-hand quarter moves to the opposite corner, the dot in the top right-hand quarter moves one corner anti-clockwise at each stage, the dot in the bottom left-hand quarter moves between the top two corners, and the dot in the bottom right-hand quarter moves one corner clockwise at each stage

21. C: the first three arcs are being repeated; and the position of the arc shifts 180°

22. EXPAND, REDUCE

23. C: looking across each line add three; looking down each column add two

24. chord, cord

25. Mary 16, George 17, Alice 24, Stephen 56, Claire 71

26. E: looking across and down, lines are carried forward from the first two squares to the final square when they appear in the same position twice in the first two squares, however, they then change from complete to broken lines, and vice versa

27. ILLICIT

28. 9: $(7 \times 9) \div (7 \times 1)$

29. FOLLOWER, DISCIPLE

30.

The white dot moves corner/side/corner anti-clockwise and the black dot does the same clockwise.

31. elicit: the following word begins with the last two letters of the previous word reversed

32. pentagon

33. 9

34. A: looking across the squares, the top left corner alternates one line/two lines/three lines; the top right corner alternates line right vertical/line left vertical; the bottom left corner alternates top horizontal/bottom horizontal and the bottom right corner alternates diagonal between opposite corners

35. 5/8 or 0.625 or 62.5 per cent

36. F

37. HIBERNATE

38. 1: work backwards from 120; that is, 120 – 60 – 12 – 3 – 1

39. D: all lines are continued, however, wavy lines become straight and vice versa

40. 52: start at the top left corner and work along the top line, then back along the second line, etc, adding nine then deducting three

Test Five: Questions

1. Which is the odd one out?

2. Which word in brackets is most opposite in meaning to the word in capitals?

   REVERENT (candid, lucid, cheeky, content, culpable)

3. Identify two words (one from each set of brackets) that have a connection (analogy) with the words in capitals and relate to them in the same way.

   COCHLEA (shell, ear, brain)

   CEREBELLUM (heart, nose, brain)

4. Which number is the odd one out?

   3647 2536 5869 6957 1425 4758

5.

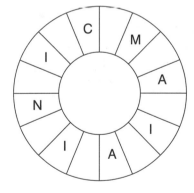

   Read clockwise to find a 16-letter word. Only alternate letters have been shown, and you have to find the starting point.

6. How many lines appear below?

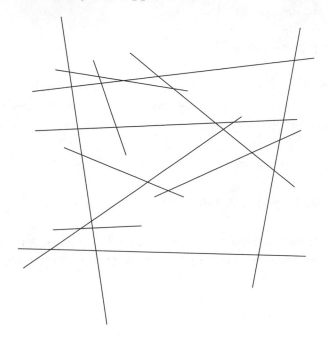

7. 0, 1, 2, 5, 20, 25, ?, ?

What two numbers should replace the question marks?

8. Which is the odd one out?

exacerbate, alleviate, amplify, escalate, inflate

9.

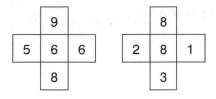

What number should replace the question mark?

10. The name of which creature can be placed on the bottom row to complete seven three-letter words reading downwards?

D A S A M Y W

U R A G A O A

* * * * * * *

11.

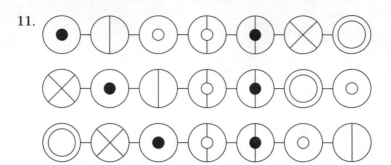

What comes next?

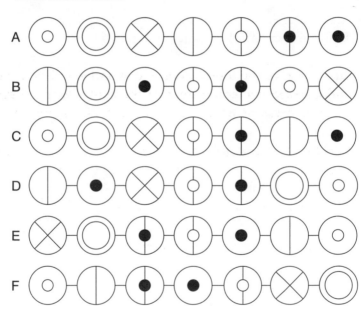

12.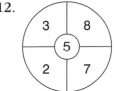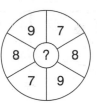

What number should replace the question mark?

13.

	N	E
A	M	T
M		I

Start at one of the four corner letters and spiral clockwise round the perimeter, finishing at the centre letter to spell out a nine-letter word. You must provide the missing letters.

14. In eight years time the combined age of me and my two sons will be 124. What will it be in five years time?

15. Which two words are closest in meaning?

old, stiff, ripe, pure, uniform, mellow

16.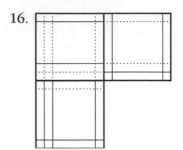

Which is the missing tile?

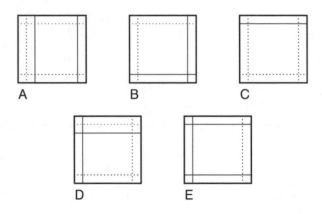

17. abyss is to chasm as fissure is to: crevice, recess, gorge, canyon, opening

18. Jack is twice as old as Jill, but in five years time he will only be one and a half times as old. How old are Jack and Jill now?

19. Change one letter only in each of the words below to produce a familiar phrase:

    HOME SO LINE

20. 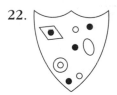 ?

Draw the missing figure in the above sequence.

21. 1000, 865, ?, 595, 460, 325

What number should replace the question mark?

22.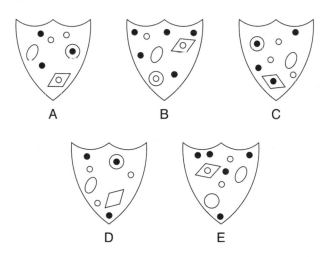

Which shield below has most in common with the shield above?

23. Identify two words that sound alike, but are spelled differently, which mean:

    potency
    small insect

24.

14	26	28
91	18	89
57	177	22
189	16	7

Multiply the lowest even number in the grid by the highest odd number.

25. What is the meaning of laconic?

    dull, uninspiring
    tearful
    using few words
    emotionally unstable
    sarcastic

26.

 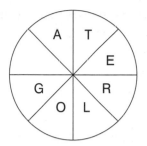

Work clockwise round each circle to spell out two eight-letter words that are synonymous. You have to find the starting points and provide the missing letters.

27. 17, 4, 29, 13, 41, 22, 53, 31, ?

What number should replace the question mark?

28.

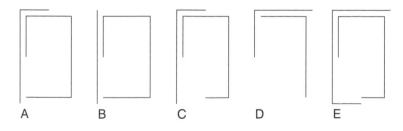

What comes next?

A   B   C   D   E

29.

	T	I
E		M
T	N	O

Spiral clockwise round the perimeter and finish at the centre square to spell out a nine-letter word. You must find the starting point and provide the missing letters.

30.

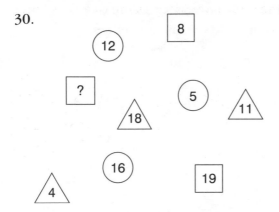

What number should replace the question mark?

31.

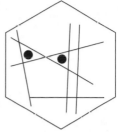

To which hexagon below can a dot be added so that *both* dots then meet the same conditions as the two dots in the hexagon above?

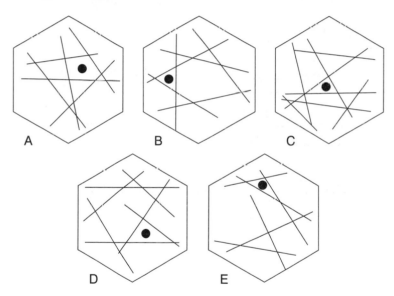

32.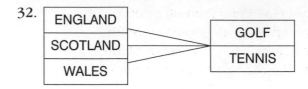

Three teams, from England, Scotland and Wales, are competing for two trophies, one for golf and one for tennis. How many different outcomes of the two competitions exist?

6, 8, 9, or 12?

33. Which is the odd one out?

statement, fluster, retirement, restful, testament

34. Switch A turns lights 1 and 2 on/off or off/on
    Switch B turns lights 2 and 4 on/off or off/on
    Switch C turns lights 1 and 3 on/off or off/on
    Switch D turns lights 3 and 4 on/off or off/on

    ● = ON

    ○ = OFF

    Switches B, D, A and C are thrown in turn with the result that Figure 1 turns into Figure 2. Which switch does not work at all?

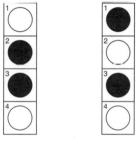

Figure 1   Figure 2

35.

5	7	4	3	1
1	2	2	6	5
6	6	5	?	
1	2			

What number should replace the question mark?

36.

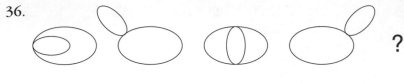

What comes next?

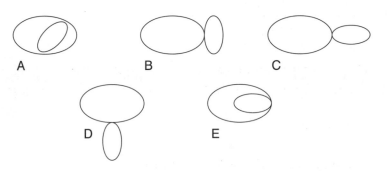

37. Find two words (7, 4) in this diagram. Letters are traced across the circle by chords. If the next letter is four letters or less away, it will be found by tracing around the circumference. Clue: may be difficult to swim over.

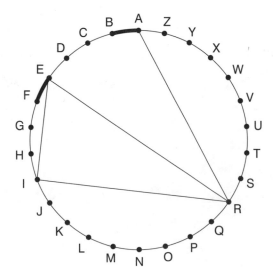

38.

A	B	C	D	E	
F	G	H	I	J	
K	L	M	N	O	
P	Q	R	S	T	
U	V	W	X	Y	Z

What letter is immediately to the left of the letter that is immediately below the letter two to the left of the letter I?

39. Which number is the odd one out?

3861 8712 5247 4356 1485 3645

40.

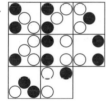

Which is the missing tile?

A   B   C   D   E   F   G   H

Test Five: Answers

1. C: it has three white and one black on the left and three black and one white on the right. The rest are the opposite way round.

2. cheeky

3. ear, brain

4. 6957: all the rest progress +3, –2, +3

5. CIRCUMNAVIGATION

6. 12

7. 150, 157: the sequence progresses +1, ×2, +3, ×4, +5, ×6, +7

8. alleviate: it means to lessen, the rest meaning to increase

9. 4: (6 + 7) – (4 + 5)

10. OCTOPUS: to produce DUO, ARC, SAT, AGO, MAP, YOU, WAS

11. C: at each stage the third circle moves to the end and the sixth circle moves to the beginning

12. 8: the number in the middle is the average of the numbers round the outside. So, $7 + 8 + 9 + 7 + 8 + 9 = 48$, and $48 \div 6 = 8$

13. MAGNETISM

14. 109: in five years we will each be three years younger than in eight years, $5 \times 3 = 15$, and $124 - 15 = 109$

15. ripe, mellow

16. C: all lines carry on and change from dotted to unbroken, and vice versa

17. crevice

18. Jack 10 and Jill 5

19. COME TO LIFE

20.

    The sequence progresses circle, triangle, diamond, with alternate horizontal/vertical lines.

21. 730: deduct 135 each time

22. C: it contains four black dots and three white

23. might/mite

24. 2646 (14 × 189)

25. using few words

26. SATURATE, WATERLOG

27. 65: there are two alternate sequences: +12 and +9

28. C: the large rectangle is being dismantled, half a side at a time anti-clockwise; the small rectangle is being constructed half a side at a time clockwise

29. TESTIMONY

30. 6: so that the numbers in the triangles, squares and circles add up to 33

31. C: so that one dot appears in one triangle and the other dot appears in two triangles (in the example the right-hand side forms a small triangle and a larger triangle and the dot is in both)

32. 9: the alternatives are:

    England win both golf and tennis
    Scotland win both golf and tennis
    Wales win both golf and tennis
    England win golf, Scotland win tennis
    Scotland win golf, England win tennis
    England win golf, Wales win tennis
    Wales win golf, England win tennis
    Scotland win golf, Wales win tennis
    Wales win golf, Scotland win tennis

33. retirement: statement/testament and fluster/restful are anagram pairs

34. Switch A is faulty.

35. 2: so that each square block of four numbers totals 15

36. E: the small ellipse moves 45° clockwise and alternates inside/outside of the larger ellipse

37. BARRIER REEF

38. K

39. 3645: in all the others the number formed by the first two digits added to the number formed by the second two digits equals 99

40. B: looking across and down, only dots that appear in the same position in the first two squares are carried forward to the third square, however, they then change from black to white and vice versa

Test Six: Questions

1.

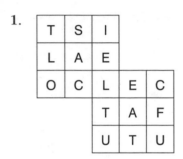

Each square contains the letters of a nine-letter word. Find the two words that are similar in meaning.

2. 1, 3, 4, 7, 11, 18, 29, ?

What number should replace the question mark?

3. Which four bits can be joined together to form two words that have opposite meanings?

ant, ert, uce, ire, ill, and, red, tic, exp

4.

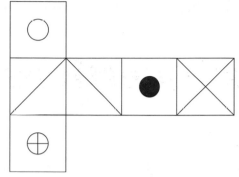

When the above is folded to form a cube, which is the only one of the following that *can* be produced?

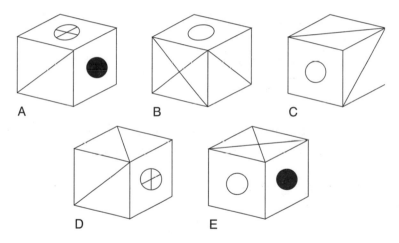

5.   blanch is to boil as sauté is to: simmer, fry, soak, roast, garnish

6.   In a game of eight players lasting for 70 minutes, six substitutes alternate with each player. This means that all players, including the substitutes, are on the pitch for the same length of time. For how long?

7. If 2 = H are BTO is two heads are better than one, what is the meaning of 2 = S to ES?

8. Which three of the four pieces below can be fitted together to form a perfect square?

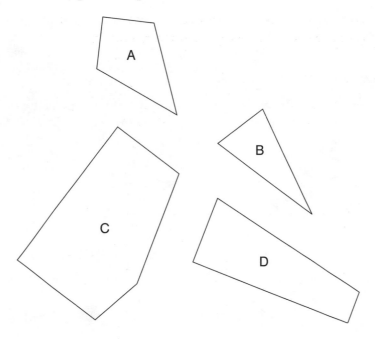

9. Which is the odd one out?

   parabolic, lancet, abutment, trefoil, ogee

10.

8	3	4
9	4	6
12	2	?

Look at lines both across and down and work out what number should replace the question mark?

11.

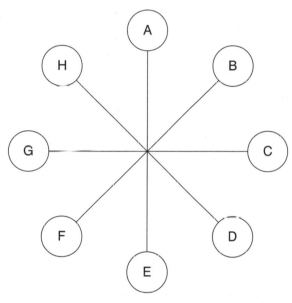

What letter is directly opposite the letter two places anti-clockwise away from the letter directly opposite the letter H?

12.

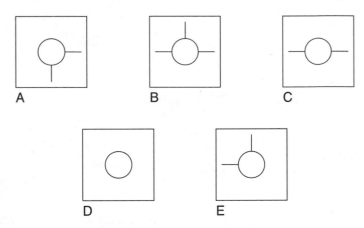

Which is the missing tile?

A   B   C

D   E

13. Change one letter only in each of the words below to produce a familiar phrase:

SO LID ON WANT

14. Insert the numbers 1–5 in the circles so that for any particular circle the sum of the numbers in the circles connected directly to it equals the value corresponding to the number in that circle as given in the list.

Example: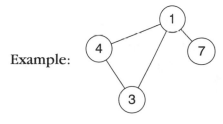

1 = 14 (4 + 3 + 7)
3 = 5 (4 + 1)
4 = 4 (1 + 3)
7 = 1

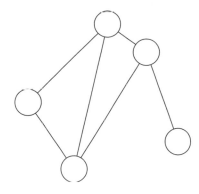

1 = 4
2 = 12
3 = 7
4 = 8
5 = 9

15.

	A	
O	C	I
N	A	P

Start at one of the four corner letters and spiral clockwise round the perimeter, finishing at the centre letter to spell out a nine-letter word. You must provide the missing letters.

16.

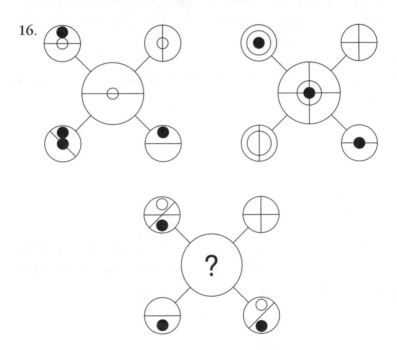

Which circle should replace the question mark?

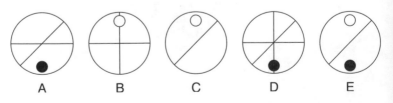

A	B	C	D	E

17.

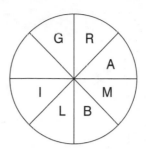

Find two eight-letter words reading clockwise in each circle. The words are antonyms. You have to find the starting point of each word, and provide the missing letter.

18. Which of the following is not an anagram of a type of building?

delta arch
raiment
cleats
the Arctic
a blowgun

19. If five men can build a house in 16 days, how long will it take just two men to build the same house, assuming all men work at the same rate?

20.

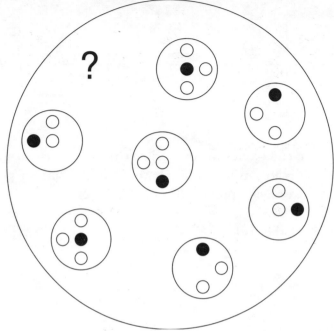

Which circle should replace the question mark?

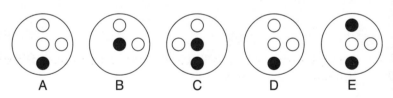

21.

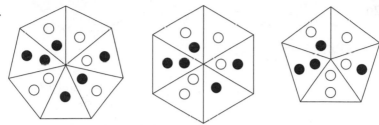

What comes next?

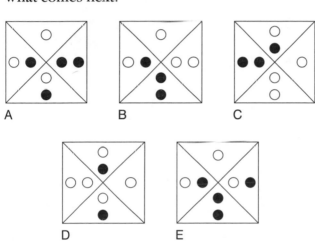

22. Change one letter only in each word to produce a familiar phrase:

cone do line

23. IQS: LNV
JRM: ?

LOP, MOP, LIP, MOW or KIP?

33749

24. 742 (8710) 138
    395 (12167) 972
    819 (?) 356

    What number should replace the question mark?

25. FAIRER BEETLE is an anagram of which two words that
    are similar in meaning?

26.

    Which hexagon below has most in common with the
    hexagon above?

A

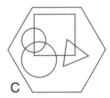

B

C

D

E

27. Identify two words that sound alike but are spelled differently, which mean:

    regrets
    artifice

28. Simplify:

$$\frac{27}{74} \div \frac{9}{37} \times \frac{6}{17}$$

    to the lowest fraction.

29.

A	B	C	D	E
F	G	H	I	J
K	L	M	N	O
P	Q	R	S	T
U	V	W	X	Y	Z

What letter is two letters to the right of the letter two letters above the letter four letters to the left of the letter Z?

30.

Draw the missing figure in the above sequence.

31.

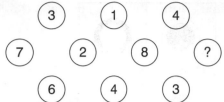

What number should replace the question mark?

32. night long boat house ?

What comes next?

calm, hold, panic, wind, post

33. rifle is to firearm as cutlass is to: blade, sword, weapon, steel, sever

34.

6	7	9	16
4	3	2	4
6	11	5	32
18	10	13	?

What number should replace the question mark?

35.

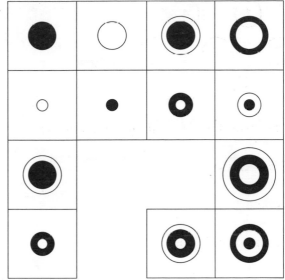

Which is the missing section?

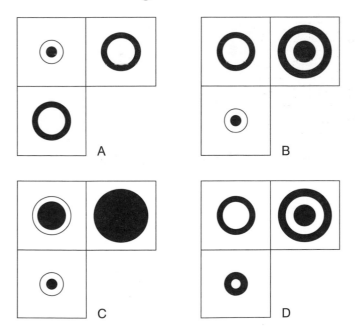

36. 7 4 2 6 3 5 8 1 9

    What is the difference between the average of the numbers above and the second lowest even number?

37. How much does a bag of flour weigh if it weighs 1 kilogram plus the weight of half the bag of flour?

38. Fill in the missing letters to find two types of tree:

    *U*A*Y****

    *A*D*L*O**

39.

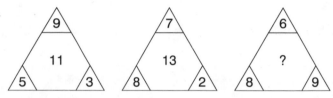

    What number should replace the question mark?

40.

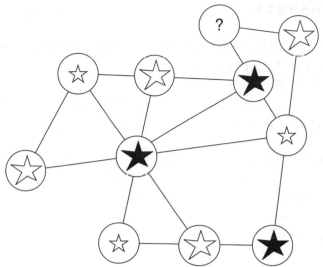

Which is missing?

A

B

C

Test Six: Answers

1. OSCILLATE, FLUCTUATE

2. 47: each number is the sum of the previous two numbers i.e. 18 + 29 = 47

3. expand, reduce

4. E

5. fry

6. 40 minutes: $(70 \times 8) \div 14$

   Total time for eight players = $70 \times 8 = 560$ minutes. However, as 14 people are each on the pitch for an equal length of time, they are each on the pitch for 40 minutes $(560 \div 14)$.

7. two sides to every story

8.

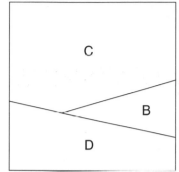

9. abutment: it is part of a structure, the rest are specific types of arch

10. 4: in each row and column in order to arrive at the final number multiply the first two numbers together and divide by 6

11. F

12. D: looking both across and down, only lines that appear in both the first two squares are carried forward to the third square

13. TO LIE IN WAIT

14.

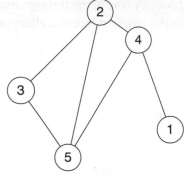

15. PANORAMIC

16. C: only lines and symbols that appear just twice in the outer circles appear in the inner circle

17. SUCCINCT, RAMBLING

18. the Arctic = architect

    The buildings are:
    cathedral (delta arch)
    minaret (raiment)
    castle (cleats)
    bungalow (a blowgun)

19. 40 days: five men take $5 \times 16 = 80$ man days to build the house. Two men will, therefore, take 40 days to build the house ($80 \div 2$).

20. A: each pair of circles are mirror images of each other

21. E: the number of sides reduces by one at each stage, and the section two clockwise from the single white dot disappears

22. come to life

23. MOP

    JklM – RqpO – MnoP

24. 11615: 8 + 3 = 11; 1 + 5 = 6; 9 + 6 = 15

25. FREE, LIBERATE

26. C: the two circles overlap each other and the square; the triangle and square overlap

27. rues/ruse

28. $\dfrac{27}{74} \times \dfrac{37}{9} \times \dfrac{6}{17} = \dfrac{3}{2} \times \dfrac{6}{17} = \dfrac{18}{34} = \dfrac{9}{17}$

29. N

30.

    At each stage lines are added to a new corner working anti-clockwise and a new line is added to corners already containing a line.

31. 6: 36 × 2 = 72; 14 × 2 = 28 and 43 × 2 = 86

32. hold: to form compound words: nightlong, longboat, boathouse, household

33. sword

34. 32:

$$6 \times 4 = 6 + 18$$
$$7 \times 3 = 11 + 10$$
$$9 \times 2 = 5 + 13$$
$$16 \times 4 = 32 + 32$$

35. B: looking across and down add another circle, alternating black/white, to alternate squares

36. 1: average $45 \div 9 = 5$; second lowest even number $= 4$

37. 2 kilograms: half weight $= 1$kg $(+1$kg$) = 2$kg

38. EUCALYPTUS, SANDALWOOD

39. 5: $(6 + 8) - 9$

40. B: so that each connected straight line of three circles contains one each of the three different types of star

Test Seven: Questions

1.

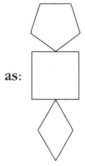 is to:

as:

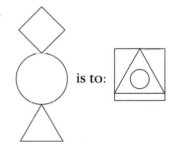

is to:

A   B   C   D   E

2. Which is the odd one out?

    banner, staff, pennant, streamer, oriflamme

3. Peter, Paul and Mary share out a certain sum of money between them. Peter gets ⅖, Paul gets 0.55 and Mary gets £45.00. How much is the original sum of money?

4.

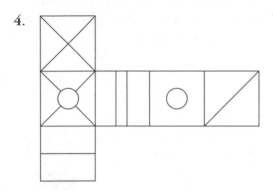

When the above is folded to form a cube, which is the only one of the following that *can* be produced?

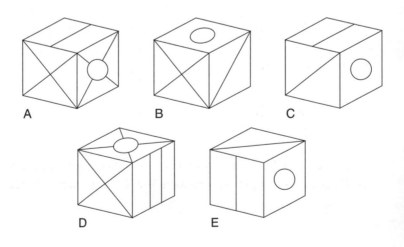

5. Which word in brackets is closest in meaning to the word in capitals?

   INTRINSIC (precursory, interfering, obstinate, elemental, fascinating)

6. Place a four-letter word inside the brackets that will complete a word or phrase when tacked onto the word on the left, and will form another word or phrase when placed in front of the word on the right.

   HEAD (****) LASS

7.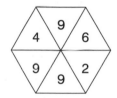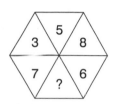

   What number should replace the question mark?

8.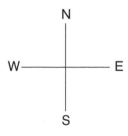

   Find the starting point and visit every square once each to finish at the treasure marked T. 1N 2W means 1 North, 2 West.

9.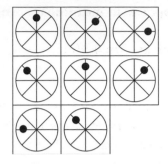

Which is the missing tile?

A   B   C   D   E

10.

20	19	18	17	16
31	28	?	22	19
26	21	16	?	6
26	22	18	14	?

Which is the missing section?

A

B

C

D

11. Which two words are most opposite in meaning?

    lucrative, proficient, decorous, unskilled, unusual, industrious

12. Identify two words (one from each set of brackets) that have a connection (analogy) with the words in capitals and relate to them in the same way.

    EMBARK (sail, venture, develop)

    INAUGURATE (speech, invent, introduce)

13. Which number is the odd one out?

    571219

    461016

    831114

    461016

    971613

    781523

14. The following clue leads to which pair of rhyming words?

    yank yarn

15.

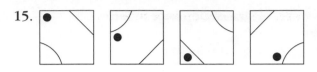

What comes next in the above sequence?

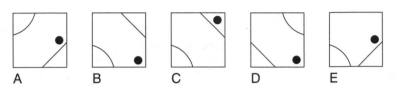

16. 100, 97.25, 91.75, 83.5, ?

What number should replace the question mark?

17. dentiform is to tooth as dendriform is to: triangle, tree, doughnut, arch, foot

18. The average of three numbers is 48. The average of two of these numbers is 56. What is the third number?

19. Arrange the three-letter bits below into the correct order to spell out a familiar saying:

nwo ion der tha eak rds lou ssp act

20. How many different size circles appear below?

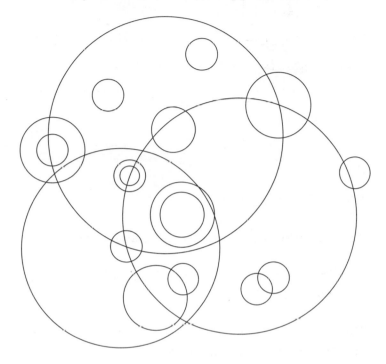

21. What is the longest word in the English language that can be produced out of the set of letters below? Letters may only be used once in the word so produced.

MEOIALJTBG

22. The letters below represent a phrase where the initial letters of each word and the spaces have been removed. What is the phrase?

USHHEOATUT

23.

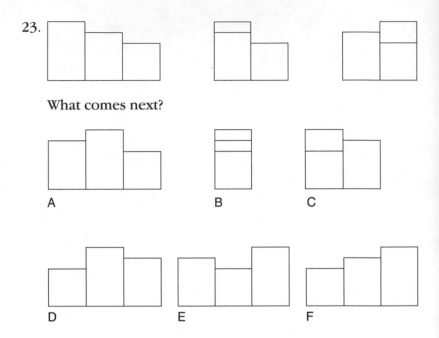

What comes next?

A   B   C

D   E   F

24. 71, 81, 74, 77, 77, 73, 80, 69, ?

What number should replace the question mark?

25. Place a word in the bracket that forms a new word or phrase when tacked onto the word on the left, and another word or phrase when placed in front of the word on the right.

home (　　　　) fast

26.

5	2		
		9	1
3			9
	8	1	

Insert the remaining numbers below into the grid so that each line across and down totals 21.

6 6 6
5 5 8
7 3

27.

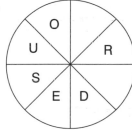 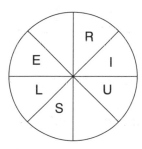

Find the starting point and work anti-clockwise round each circle to find two types of creature, each eight letters long. You have to provide the missing letters.

28.

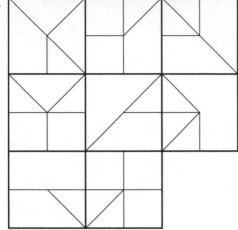

Which is the missing tile?

A

B

C

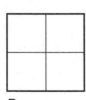

D

E

F

29.

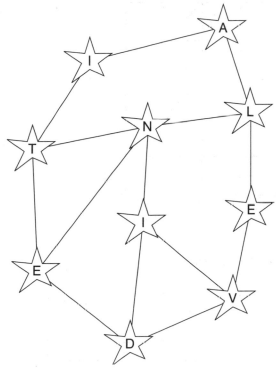

Move from star to star along connecting lines to spell out a 10-letter word. All letters are used once each only.

30.

 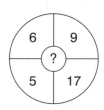

What number should replace the question mark?

31.

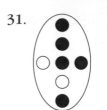 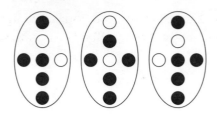

Which is missing?

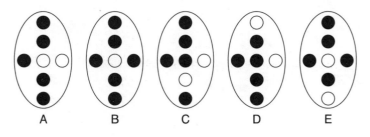

32.

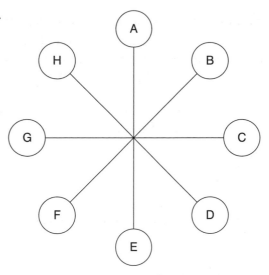

What letter is directly opposite the letter that is two letters away clockwise from the letter that is directly opposite the letter that is three letters away anti-clockwise from the letter E?

33. In 13 years time the combined ages of my three brothers will be 94. What will it be in nine years time?

34.

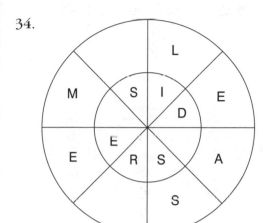

Find two words, one reading clockwise round the outer circle, and one reading anti-clockwise round the inner circle, which are opposite in meaning. You must provide the missing letters.

35.

	7		8		12	
2	21	8	35	8	?	?
	4		11		7	

What numbers should replace the question marks?

36.

Which shield below has most in common with the shield above?

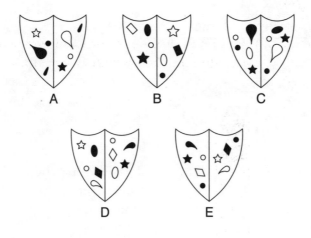

37. Switch A turns lights 1 and 2 on/off or off/on
    Switch B turns lights 2 and 4 on/off or off/on
    Switch C turns lights 1 and 3 on/off or off/on
    Switch D turns lights 3 and 4 on/off or off/on

    ● = ON

    ○ = OFF

    Switches C, A, D and B are thrown in turn with the result
    that Figure 1 turns into Figure 2. Which switch does not
    work at all?

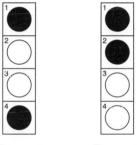

    Figure 1   Figure 2

38.

A	P	B		
E	T	L		
A	A	L	S	S
		T	E	T
		A	S	E

    Each square contains the letters of a nine-letter word.
    Find the two nine-letter words that are antonyms.

39.

5	7	4	9	8	2	7
3	8	6	4	7	5	9
9	6	1	4	5	8	?

What number should replace the question mark?

40.

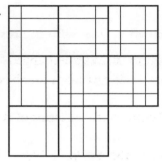

Which is the missing tile?

A   B   C   D   E

Test Seven: Answers

1. A: the square goes inside the diamond and the diamond in turn goes inside the pentagon, which turns onto its base

2. staff: it is a support for a flag. The rest are all types of flag.

3. £900: change everything to twentieths. So, $\frac{8}{20} + \frac{11}{20} = \frac{19}{20}$. Therefore, £45.00 must be equal to $\frac{1}{20}$ and original sum of money must be $45 \times 20 = 900$.

4. C

5. elemental

6. WIND: HEADWIND and WINDLASS

7. 1: the number formed at the top is half of the number formed at the bottom i.e. $358 \times 2 = 716$

8.

5	3	7
8	6	2
1	9	4

The above numbers indicate the order in which the nine squares should be visited from the starting point (the square numbered 1) through to the finishing point (the treasure square number 9).

9. B: looking across, the dot moves 45° clockwise at each stage, but looking down it moves 45° anti-clockwise

10. A: lines across progress, in turn, –1, –3, –5, –4

11. proficient, unskilled

12. venture, introduce

13. 971613: numbers are obtained by adding pairs of digits i.e. with 571219: 5 + 7 = 12; 7 + 12 = 19. To follow this same pattern 971613 would have to be 971623.

14. pull wool

15. B: the dot moves corner/side anti-clockwise, the straight line and the curved line both move corner to corner clockwise

16. 72.5: the amount deducted increases by 2.75 each time i.e. 2.75, 5.5, 8.25, 11

17. tree

18. 32: the total of three numbers must be $48 \times 3 = 144$. The total of two numbers must be $56 \times 2 = 112$. Therefore, $144 - 112 = 32$.

19. actions speak louder than words

20. 6

21. OBLIGATE

22. PUSH THE BOAT OUT

23. E: the rectangle starting on the left is moving from left to right one place at a time at each stage

24. 83: there are two alternate sequences: $+3$ and -4

25. stead: to give homestead and steadfast

26.

5	2	8	6
6	5	9	1
3	6	3	9
7	8	1	5

27. DORMOUSE and SQUIRREL

28. F: looking across and down, lines are carried forward from the first two squares to the final square, except where two lines appear in the same position in the first two squares, in which case they are cancelled out

29. EVIDENTIAL

30. 9: $(6 + 17) - (5 + 9)$

31. B: the white dots are each moving left to right and bottom to top (and vice versa) one place at a time at each stage

32. D

33. 82:

    Combined age in 9 years time will be $94 - (3 \times (13 - 9))$.

34. ASSEMBLE, DISPERSE

35. 31 and 4: $12 \times 7 = 84$; $8 + 12 + 7 + 4 = 31$

36. B: the left side contains the same symbols as the right side but with black/white reversal

37. Switch B is faulty.

38. PALATABLE, TASTELESS

39. 6: $5749827 + 3864759 = 9614586$

40. E: looking across and down, lines are carried forward from the first two squares to the final square, except where two lines appear in the same position in the first two squares, in which case they are cancelled out

Test Eight: Questions

1. 0, 1, 3, 6, 7, 9, 12, 13, 15, 18, ?, ?, ?

   What numbers should replace the question marks?

2. Find two words that differ only by the omission of a single letter (for example, place/pace), in answer to the following clue:

   bowl-shaped cavity/provide food

3.

43	6	16	12	24
2	22	1	4	9
46	30	48	5	13
38	8	36	7	3
11	20	14	10	15

   What number in the grid is three places away from itself less two, two places away from itself divided by two, three places away from itself less five and three places away from itself multiplied by three?

4.

A	C	F
E	?	J
J	L	?

Which is the missing section?

A   B   C   D

5.

To which of the squares below can a dot be added so that the dot then meets the same conditions as the dot in the square above?

A   B   C   D   E

6. Complete the following to create a palindromic phrase i.e. one that reads the same forwards and backwards, such as Madam I'm Adam.

*U**L* ***P **

Clue: scholarly errors!

7. 83 64 45 ??
    96 65 34 ??

What numbers should replace the question marks?

8.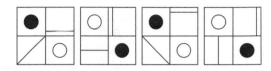

Draw the missing figure in the above sequence.

9. Which is the odd one out?

   sow, bull, buck, boar, stallion

10. The ages of five family members total 107 between them.

   The ages of Margaret and Stuart total 29 between them.
   The ages of Stuart and Jeffrey total 44 between them.
   The ages of Jeffrey and Brian total 57 between them.
   The ages of Brian and Philip total 46 between them.

   How old is each family member?

11. IVY CITRATE is an anagram of which two 10-letter words in the English language?

12.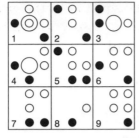

Looking at lines across and down, if the first two tiles are combined to produce the third tile, with the exception that like symbols are cancelled out, which of the above tiles is incorrect, and with which of the tiles below should it be replaced?

A   B   C   D   E

13. Which two words are most opposite in meaning?

watertight, humid, tractable, opulent, portentous, tenuous

14.

7	6	5	7	6	3
4	9	2	8	1	9
1	3	7	3	2	7
3	8	4	9	9	5
5	4	2	3	2	?

What number should replace the question mark?

15. Add three consecutive letters of the alphabet to the group of letters below, without splitting the consecutive letters of the alphabet, to form another word.

    GERE

16.

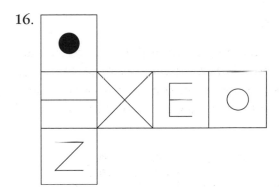

When the above is folded to form a cube, which is the only one of the following that *can* be produced?

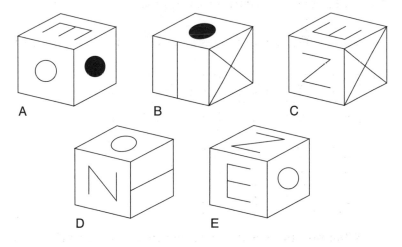

17. closed is to shut as open is to: obscure, visible, field, overt, wide

18. Harry is one and a third as old as Larry and Larry is one and a third as old as Carrie. Together their ages total 74. How old are Larry, Harry and Carrie?

19. Which two words are closest in meaning?

    salubrious, healthy, identical, conspicuous, devout, bleak

20.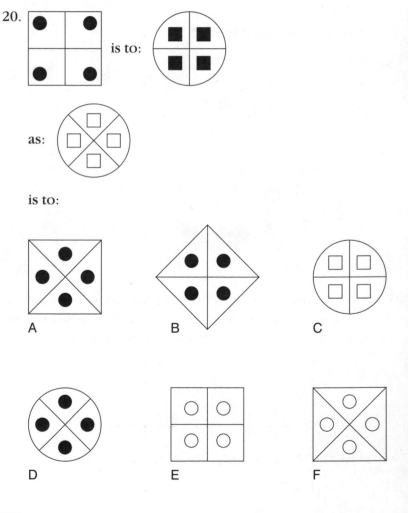

21.

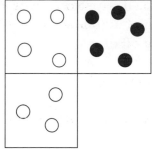

Which is the missing tile?

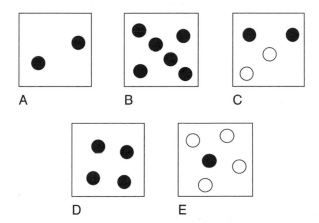

A   B   C

D   E

22. Find two words, both reading clockwise round each circle. You must find the starting point of each word and provide the missing letters. The two words form a phrase.

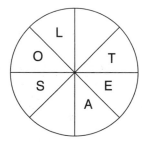
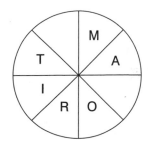

23. Switch A turns lights 1 and 2 on/off or off/on
    Switch B turns lights 2 and 4 on/off or off/on
    Switch C turns lights 1 and 3 on/off or off/on
    Switch D turns lights 3 and 4 on/off or off/on

     = ON

    ○ = OFF

    Switches A, C, D and B are thrown in turn with the result that Figure 1 turns into Figure 2. Which switch does not work at all?

    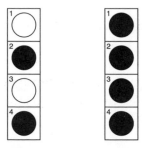

    Figure 1   Figure 2

24.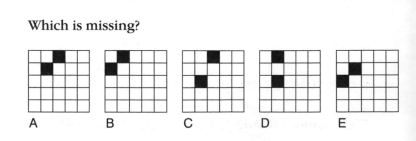

    Which is missing?

    A   B   C   D   E

25. The letters below represent a phrase where the initial letters of each word and the spaces have been removed. What is the phrase?

    INEFORK

26.

23	24	41
57	92	91
18	16	28
56	21	19

    Multiply the highest odd number in the grid by the lowest even number.

27. Only one group of five letters below can be rearranged to spell out a five-letter word in the English language. Identify the word.

    LEVUR

    TNIEC

    HEOLC

    ANOIP

    IRNAL

28. 1, 2.25, 3.75, 5.5, 7.5, 9.75, ?

    What number should replace the question mark?

29. Place a word in the bracket that forms a new word or phrase when tacked onto the word on the left, and another word or phrase when placed in front of the word on the right.

second (   ) some

30.

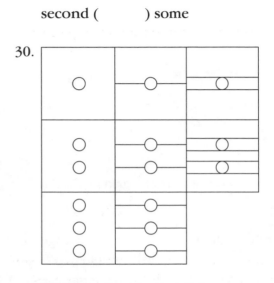

Which is the missing tile?

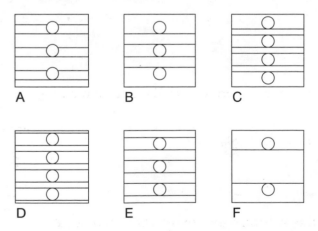

31. How many minutes is it before midnight if 32 minutes ago it was three times as many minutes past 22.00?

32. boater, nail, about, ruin, alibi, ?

    Which word below comes next in the above sequence?

    stray, tiara, treat, suit, trail

33.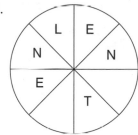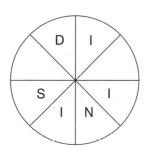

    Work clockwise round the circles to spell out two eight-letter words that are antonyms. Each word commences in a different circle, and you must find the starting point of each. Every letter is used once each and all letters are consecutive.

34. 1, 31, 59, 85, 109, ?

    What number should replace the question mark?

35.

    Draw the missing figure in the above sequence.

36.

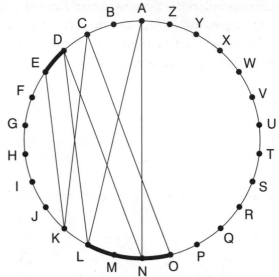

Find two words (4, 6) in this diagram. Letters are traced across the circle by chords. If the next letter is four letters or less away, it will be found by tracing around the circumference. Clue: no coastline

37.

E	L	I
	F	E
	I	D

Start at one of the four corner letters and spiral clockwise round the perimeter, finishing at the centre letter to spell out a nine-letter word. You must provide the missing letters.

38. What is $\dfrac{5}{9}$ divided by $\dfrac{15}{18}$?

39. Three coins are tossed in the air and two of the coins land with heads face upwards. What are the chances on the next toss of the coins that at least two of the coins will land with heads face upwards again?

40.

Which shield below has most in common with the shield above?

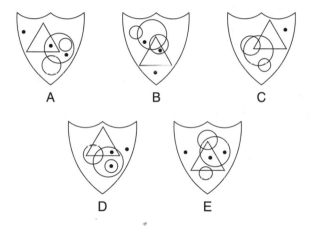

165

Test Eight: Answers

1. 19, 21, 24: the sequence progresses +1, +2, +3 repeated

2. crater/cater

3. 8

4. B: looking across, the letters jump +2, +3 in the alphabet, for example – AbCdeF. Looking down, they progress +4, +5, for example – AbcdEfghiJ.

5. D: so the dot appears in the diamond and circle only

6. PUPILS SLIP UP

7. 2 6
    0 3

    Looking across, the numbers in the same position in each pair progress: 8, 6, 4, 2; 3, 4, 5, 6; 9, 6, 3, 0; 6, 5, 4, 3

8.

The top left-hand corner alternates black dot/white dot; the top right-hand corner alternates horizontal line/vertical line; the bottom left-hand corner line moves diagonal/vertical/diagonal/horizontal/diagonal, and the bottom right-hand corner alternates white dot/black dot.

9. sow: it is a female animal, the rest are male

10. Margaret 17, Stuart 12, Jeffrey 32, Brian 25 and Philip 21

11. CREATIVITY, REACTIVITY

12.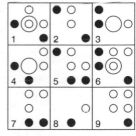

Tile 6 is incorrect and should be replaced by tile E.

13. watertight, tenuous

14. 6: the total of the numbers in each column alternates 20, 30, 20, 30, 20, 30

15. GESTURE

16. A

17. overt

18. Harry 32, Larry 24, Carrie 18

19. salubrious, healthy

20. F: the circle becomes a square and the four white squares become white circles

21. D: looking across, the number of dots increases by one and white becomes black. Looking down, the number of dots decreases by one and the dots stay the same colour.

22. ABSOLUTE MAJORITY

23. Switch C is faulty.

24. C: the black square originally in the top right-hand corner is moving right to left one space at a time at each stage. The other black square is moving from bottom to top.

25. LINE OF WORK

26. 1456 (91 × 16)

27. ANOIP = PIANO

28. 12.25: add 1.25, 1.5, 1.75, 2, 2.25, 2.5

29. hand: second hand, handsome

30. E: looking across, the number of lines increases. Looking down, the number of circles increases by one and the circles fit within the bands formed by the lines.

31. 22 minutes. Midnight less 22 minutes = 11.38. Less 32 minutes = 11.06. 10 p.m. (22.00) plus 66 minutes (22 × 3) = 11.06.

32. tiara. The consonants b t r n and l are being repeated in the same order.

33. LENGTHEN, DIMINISH

34. 131: add 30, 28, 26, 24, 22

35.

The large circle moves 45° clockwise and alternates white/black. The centre dot alternates black/white.

36. LAND LOCKED

37. DISBELIEF

38. $\dfrac{5}{9} \times \dfrac{18}{15} = \dfrac{2}{3}$

39. 50 per cent: it is a certainty that at least two coins will land with the same side face up. It is equally likely that these two coins will land heads up as they will land tails upwards. It is immaterial what occurred in the previous toss.

40. B: it has three circles of differing sizes, one triangle, one dot out on its own, one dot in the large circle only and the other dot in the middle-sized circle and triangle.

Test Nine: Questions

1.

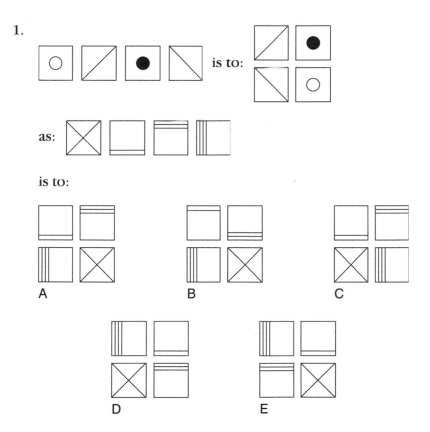

is to:

as:

is to:

A

B

C

D

E

2. VEILED HARE is an anagram of which two words that are opposite in meaning?

3. Add one letter, not necessarily the same letter, to the beginning, middle or end of the words below to find five new words all on the same theme.

    back live fan can pin

4.

1	3	5	7
4	8	?	16
7	?	19	25
10	18	?	34

Which is the missing section?

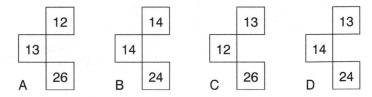

5. A B C D E F G H

    Which letter is two to the left of the letter that is four to the right of the letter immediately to the right of the letter A?

6. Which is the odd one out?

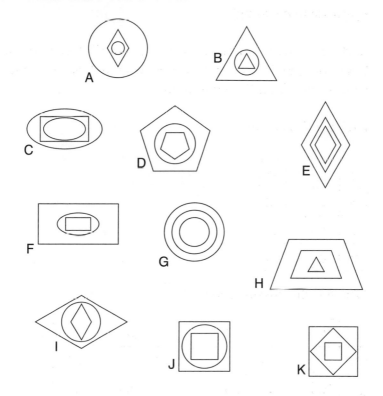

7.

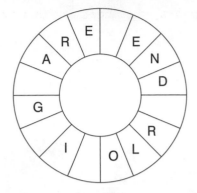

Find a familiar phrase (6, 6, 4) reading clockwise. You have to find the starting point and provide the missing letters.

8.

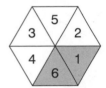 

What number should replace the question mark?

9. eastern, reality, titanic, ?

Which of the words below comes next?

natural, omnibus, include, devious or shingle

10. Which three of the pieces below, when fitted together, will form a perfect square?

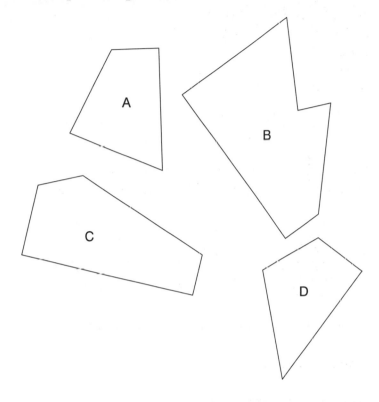

11. RASCAL MARE is an anagram of which two words that are similar in meaning?

12. gallery is to balcony as stalls is to: proscenium, stage, audience, footlights, pit

13. 3182596 is to 65283

    and 6742835 is to 53476

    therefore 7496258 is to ?

14. A, C, F, J, O, ?

    What letter comes next?

15.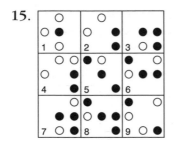

    Looking at lines across and down, if the first two tiles are combined to produce the third tile, with the exception that like symbols are cancelled out, which of the above tiles is incorrect, and with which of the tiles below should it be replaced?

    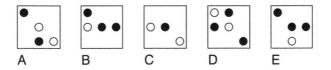

    A   B   C   D   E

16. 0, 27, 54, ?, 108, 135

    What number should replace the question mark?

17. Which is the odd one out?

    bolero, calypso, waltz, salsa, polka

18.

6	10	14	18
9	13	?	21
12	?	20	24
15	?	23	27

Which section is missing?

  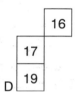

19. I met four of my old school friends today. In the morning I first saw Patricia and later bumped into Richie. Then in the afternoon I saw Christabel. Who did I encounter in the evening? Was it Thora, Stella, Thelma or Sally?

20.

When the above is folded to form a cube, which is the only one of the following that *can* be produced?

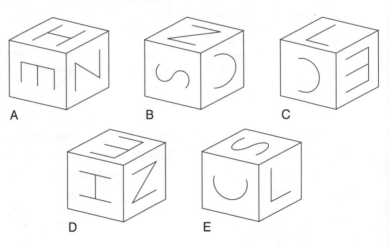

A   B   C

D   E

21.

Which shield below has most in common with the shield above?

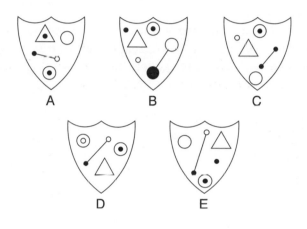

22.

7	4	5	2
5	1	9	3
2	9	1	6
?	4	3	7

What number should replace the question mark?

23.

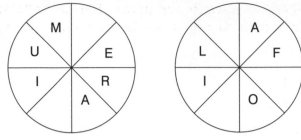

Find the starting point and work clockwise round each circle to find two types of flower, each eight letters long. You have to provide the missing letters.

24.

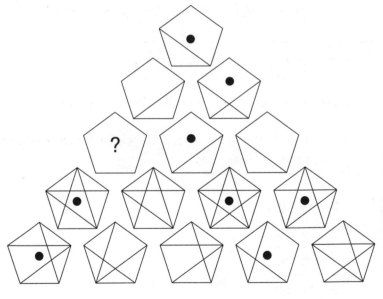

Which is missing?

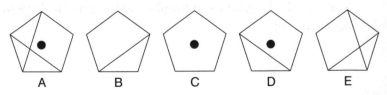

25. Using all of the letters in the phrase TOUCH VOLCANO PIECE once each only spell out the names of three types of fruit.

26.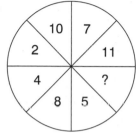

    What number should replace the question mark?

27.

    Draw the missing figure in the above sequence.

28. ASH FUEL FARM is an anagram of which two words that are opposite in meaning?

29.

171	23	18
17	19	29
78	56	27
28	71	82

    Multiply the highest even number in the grid by the lowest odd number.

30. action, effort, worth, ?, ourself

    Which of the words below is missing?

    cheer, reef, cage, rampart, idea

31.

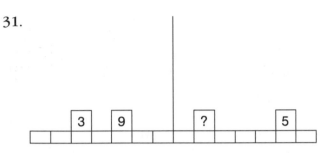

    What weight should replace the question mark in order for the scales to balance?

32.

4	9	13	5	86	2	7
82						9
79						24
6						63
35						18
1	6	37	8	49	2	?

    What number should replace the question mark?

33.

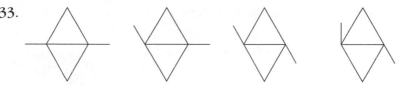

What comes next?

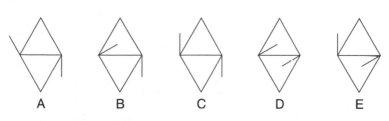

34. Place a word in the bracket that forms a new word or phrase when tacked onto the word on the left, and another word or phrase when placed in front of the word on the right.

salt (   ) fall

35. Which is the odd word out?

orders, murder, derelict, underworld, detonator

36. Stuart and Christine share out a certain sum of money in the ratio 4:5 and Christine ends up with £24.00. How much money was shared in the first place?

37. Referring again to question 36, how much money would have been shared out if the ratio had been 5:4 instead of 4:5?

38.

 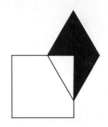 

What comes next?

A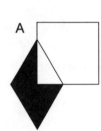

B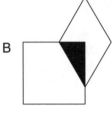

C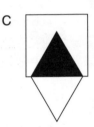

D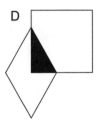

E

39.

S	I	P	Y
E	A	R	
	O	R	T

Find the starting point and work from letter to adjoining letter horizontally and vertically, but not diagonally, to spell out a 12-letter word. You have to provide the missing letters.

40.

7	9	4	5
13	11	14	9
25	27	20	23
47	45	50	43
?	?	?	?

What numbers should replace the question marks on the bottom row?

Test Nine: Answers

1. A: square 1 moves to bottom right, square 2 moves to top left, square 3 moves to top right and square 4 moves to bottom left

2. HIDE, REVEAL

3. black, olive, fawn, cyan, pink

4. A: lines across progress +2, +4, +6, + 8 in turn. Columns down progress +3, +5, +7, +9 in turn.

5. D

6. H: in all the others the outer figure is repeated in the middle

7. TENDER LOVING CARE

8. 2: the total of the numbers in the shaded section in each hexagon is half the total of the remaining numbers

9. include: each word begins with the sixth and fifth letters of the preceding word

10.

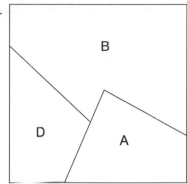

11. SCARE, ALARM

12. pit

13. 85647: reverse the first number and discard the highest and lowest digits

14. U: AbCdeFghiJklmnOpqrstU

15.

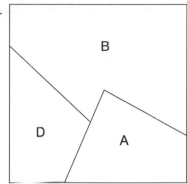

Tile 8 is incorrect and should be replaced by tile B.

16. 81: add 27 each time

17. calypso: it is a song, the rest are dances

18. B: looking across, lines progress +4, looking down, columns progress +3

19. Stella: each name begins with the middle two letters of the previous name

20. C

21. E: it contains exactly the same symbols as the original

22. 4: all lines and columns total 18

23. GERANIUM, DAFFODIL

24. C: the contents of each pentagon are determined by the contents of the two pentagons immediately below it. Lines and dots are carried forward from these two pentagons, except when a line or dot appears in the same position, in which case they are cancelled out.

25. PEACH, OLIVE, COCONUT

26. 13: opposite numbers total 15

27.

    Lines are added vertically then horizontally alternately.

28. HARMFUL, SAFE

29. 1394: (82 × 17)

30. reef: acti(**on e**)ffor(**t wo**)r(**th ree**)(**f our**)self

31.

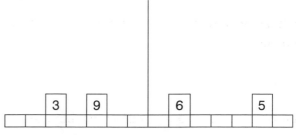

5 × 3 = 15   6 × 5 = 30
3 × 9 = 27   2 × 6 = 12
15 + 27 = 42
30 + 12 = 42

32. 5: each row of numbers contains the digits 1–9

33. C: the arms move clockwise in turn 45°

34. water: to give salt water, waterfall

35. detonator: the rest contain the letters 'der' adjacently

36. £43.20: Christine = £24 or five parts, therefore, each part = £4.80. Total of nine parts shared = £4.80 × 9 = £43.20.

37. £54.00: Christine's share = £24.00 or four parts, therefore, each part = £6.00. Total of nine parts shared = £54.00.

38. D: the diamond is moving round each corner clockwise. The black portion alternates overlapping section/diamond/square.

39. PRAISEWORTHY

40. A   B   C   D

7	9	4	5
13	11	14	9
25	27	20	23
47	45	50	43
95	97	88	93

The numbers in each row are determined, as follows, by the numbers in the row above: A + C = B; B + D = C; B + C = A; C + D = D.

Test Ten: Questions

1.

5	3
8	12
7	5

4	5
14	6
2	9

7	8
?	13
6	9

What number should replace the question mark?

2. Which word in brackets is most opposite in meaning to the word in capitals?

PALATABLE (sparse, agonising, bland, raw, inferior)

3. 100, 99.5, 98.5, 97, 95, 92.5, 89.5, ?

What number should replace the question mark?

4. Switch A turns lights 1 and 2 on/off or off/on
    Switch B turns lights 2 and 4 on/off or off/on
    Switch C turns lights 1 and 3 on/off or off/on

     = ON

     = OFF

    Switches B, A and C are thrown in turn with the result that
    Figure 1 turns into Figure 2. Which switch does not work
    at all?

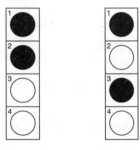

Figure 1   Figure 2

5.

To which shield below can a dot be added so that it meets the same conditions as in the shield above?

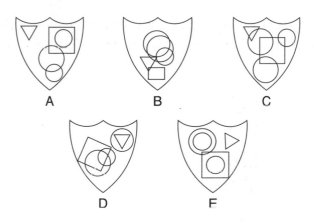

6. Which is the odd one out?

diploid, deltoid, dual, binary, twofold

7.

5	10	9	4
7	4	5	8
3	2	5	6
1	8	9	?

What number should replace the question mark?

8. Insert a pair of letters into each bracket so that they finish the word on the left and start the word on the right. The correct letters read downwards in pairs must spell out an eight-letter word.

SO (**) LT

LA (**) ST

DO (**) AL

EP (**) ON

9. Which is the odd one out?

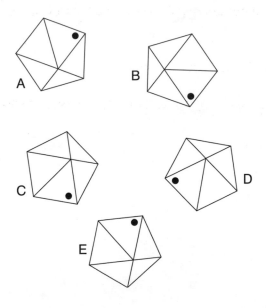

10. Which one of the following is grammatically correct?

    The father's rights activist's dog buried its bone in the garden.
    The fathers' rights activist's dog buried it's bone in the garden.
    The father's rights activist's dog buried it's bone in the garden.
    The fathers' rights' activist's dog buried its bone in the garden.
    The fathers' rights activists' dog buried it's bone in the garden.
    The fathers' rights activist's dog buried its bone in the garden.
    The father's rights activists' dog buried its bone in the garden.

11. Which number is the odd one out?

    6394, 9416, 5278, 6231, 9614, 6132, 7895, 5872, 7598

12.

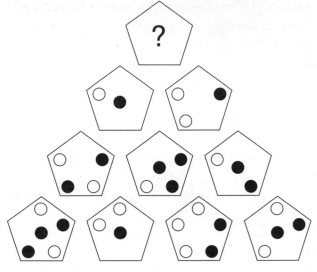

Which pentagon should replace the question mark?

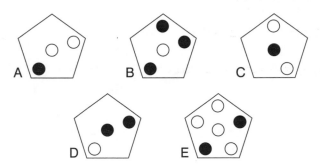

13. Which word in brackets is closest in meaning to the word in capitals?

SPARTAN (scarce, austere, erratic, limited, fierce)

14. Only one set of letters below can be rearranged into a six-letter word in the English language. Find the word.

    HURLPO

    KCIENA

    WINCAL

    EJBATC

    XELPOD

    NWIOLM

15. 7964325 is to 6975234

    and 5822139 is to 2859312

    therefore 7469851 is to ?

16.

Which shield below has most in common with the shield above?

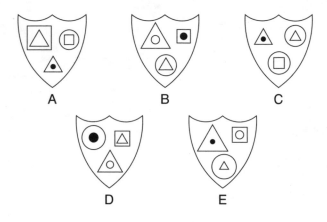

17. caster is to chair as rowel is to: wheel, spur, bicycle, pulley, gyroscope

18. Insert the numbers 1–6 in the circles so that for any particular circle the sum of the numbers in the circles connected directly to it equals the value corresponding to the numbers in that circle as given in the list.

Example: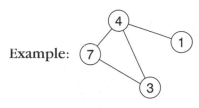

1 = 4
3 = 11 (4 + 7)
4 = 11 (1 + 3 +7)
7 = 7 (4+3)

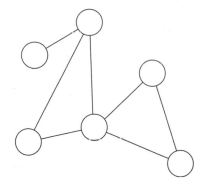

1 = 8
2 = 4
3 = 6
4 = 13
5 = 14
6 = 9

19. What four-letter word can be placed in the bracket to form a word when tacked onto the end of blue and another word when placed in front of owed?

    BLUE (****) OWED

20.

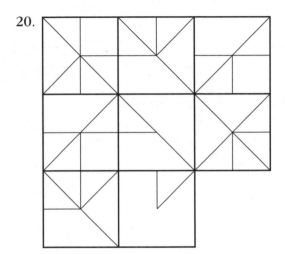

Which is the missing tile?

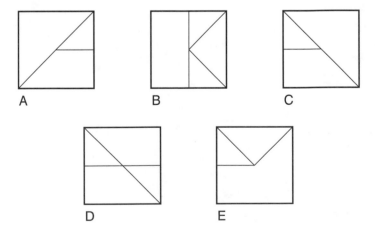

A   B   C

D   E

21.

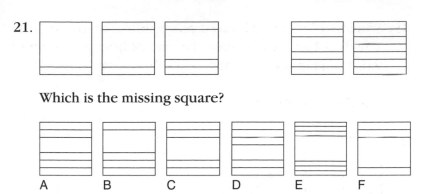

Which is the missing square?

22. Which two words are closest in meaning?

lonely, haughty, crafty, credulous, careful, arrogant

23. Switch A turns lights 1 and 2 on/off or off/on
    Switch B turns lights 2 and 4 on/off or off/on
    Switch C turns lights 1 and 3 on/off or off/on
    Switch D turns lights 3 and 4 on/off or off/on

Switches D, B, C and A are thrown in turn with the result that Figure 1 turns into Figure 2. Which switch does not work at all?

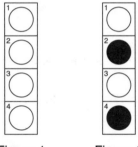

Figure 1   Figure 2

24. Using all of the letters in the phrase A CATASTROPHIC PROTON only once each spell out the names of three types of vegetable.

25.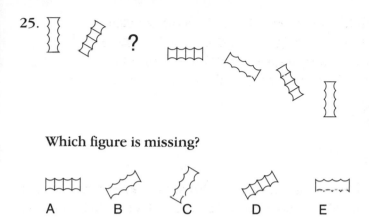

Which figure is missing?

A   B   C   D   E

26. Which two words are most opposite in meaning?

validation, revival, sarcasm, extinction, rebellion, fissure

27.

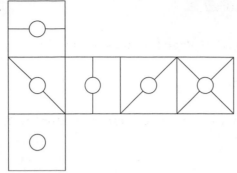

When the above is folded to form a cube, which is the only one of the following that *can* be produced?

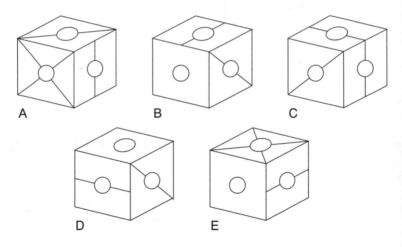

28. Which word in brackets is most opposite in meaning to the word in capitals?

SENSIBLE (unaware, subordinate, irrational, outlandish, irreverent)

29. 9, 16, 13, 13, 17, 10, 21, 7, ?

    What number should replace the question mark?

30. dirty, berry, hint, knot

    Which one word below shares a common feature with all four words above?

    part, cost, near, find, open

31. AFFIRM DEMON is an anagram of which phrase (5, 2, 4)? Clue: inclination.

32.

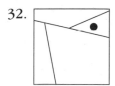

    Which square below has most in common with the square above?

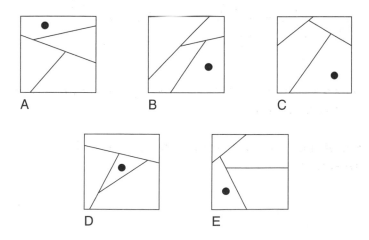

33. 70   91   120

    14   13   24

    5   7   ?

    What number should replace the question mark?

34. A B C D E F G H

    What letter is two letters to the right of the letter immediately to the left of the letter four letters to the right of the letter two letters to the left of the letter E?

35. POLLUTE SPICE is an anagram of which phrase (4, 2, 6)? Clue: demolish.

36.
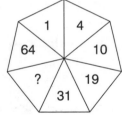

    What number should replace the question mark?

37.

To which hexagon below can a dot be added so that it then meets the same conditions as in the hexagon above?

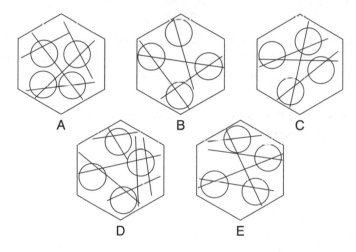

A   B   C

D   E

38. A greengrocer received a boxful of tomatoes and on opening the box found that several had gone bad. He then counted them up so that he could make a formal complaint and found that 68 were mouldy, which was 16 per cent of the total contents of the box. How many tomatoes were in the box?

39. EMPTY (PRISM) VIRUS

DEPTH (*****) DUALS

What word is coded to appear in the second bracket?

40.

What number should replace the question mark?

Test Ten: Answers

1. 17: 8 + 9 = 17; 7 + 6 = 13

2. bland

3. 86: the amount deducted increases by 0.5 each time i.e.
    0.5, 1, 1.5, 2, 2.5, 3, 3.5

4. Switch B is not working.

5. D: so that the dot is in the square and two circles

6. deltoid: it means triangular in shape. The rest mean
    double or twofold.

7. 2: in rows and columns alternate digits total the same, for
    example 5 + 9 = 10 + 4

8. METEORIC: to give some/melt, late/test, door/oral, epic/icon

9. C: the rest are the same figure rotated

10. The fathers' rights activist's dog buried its bone in the
    garden.

11. 6394: all the others are in pairs where the second and fourth digits change places: 5278/5872, 9416/9614, 7895/7598, 6231/6132

12. D: the contents of each pentagon are determined by the contents of the two pentagons immediately below it. Only when a dot appears in one of the corner positions or centre just once in these two pentagons, is it carried forward to the pentagon above.

13. austere

14. EJBATC = ABJECT

15. 6471589: reverse the first three digits, then the last four digits

16. E: it contains a triangle in a circle, a circle in a square and a black dot in a triangle

17. spur

18.

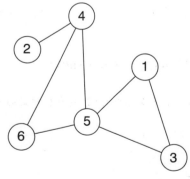

Alternatively as above but with 1 and 3 reversed.

19. BELL: BLUEBELL, BELLOWED

20. C: in each row and column the contents of the third square is determined by the contents of the first two squares. Lines are transferred from these two squares to the third square, except when they appear in the same position in both squares, in which case they are cancelled out.

21. C: a line is added at the top and bottom alternately

22. haughty, arrogant

23. Switch B is faulty.

24. SPINACH, CARROT, POTATO

25. B: the figure is tumbling over and alternates white/striped

26. revival, extinction

27. B

28. irrational

29. 25: there are two alternate sequences: +4 and −3

30. cost: all the words have their letters in alphabetical order

31. FRAME OF MIND

32. D: the dot is in a triangle

33. 5: $70 \div 14 = 5$; $91 \div 13 = 7$, $120 \div 24 = 5$

34. H

35. PULL TO PIECES

36. 46: start at 1 and work clockwise adding 3, 6, 9, 12, 15, 18

37. D: so that it appears in a circle with three secants (lines) passing through it

38. 425: (68 ÷ 16) × 100

39. PAUSE:

     5 1   (1 2 3 4 5)   3 2   4

     E M P T Y (P R I S M) V I R U S

     D E P T H (P A U S E) D U A L S

40. 13: the numbers in each circle total 100

Further Reading from Kogan Page

Books

The Advanced Numeracy Test Workbook, Mike Bryon, 2003

Aptitude, Personality and Motivation Tests: Assess Your Potential and Plan Your Career, 2nd edition, Jim Barrett, 2004

The Aptitude Test Workbook, Jim Barrett, 2003

The Graduate Psychometric Test Workbook, Mike Bryon, 2005

Great Answers to Tough Interview Questions: How to Get the Job You Want, 6th edition, Martin John Yate, 2005

How to Master Personality Questionnaires, 2nd edition, Mark Parkinson, 2000

How to Master Psychometric Tests, 3rd edition, Mark Parkinson, 2004

How to Pass Advanced Aptitude Tests, Jim Barrett, 2002

How to Pass the Civil Service Qualifying Tests, 2nd edition, Mike Bryon, 2003

How to Pass Computer Selection Tests, Sanjay Modha, 1994

How to Pass Firefighter Recruitment Tests, Mike Bryon, 2004

How to Pass Graduate Psychometric Tests, 2nd edition, Mike Bryon, 2001

How to Pass the New Police Selection System, 2nd edition, Harry Tolley, Billy Hodge and Catherine Tolley, 2004

How to Pass Numeracy Tests, 2nd edition, Harry Tolley and Ken Thomas, 2000

How to Pass Numerical Reasoning Tests, Heidi Smith, 2003

How to Pass Professional Level Psychometric Tests, 2nd edition, Sam Al-Jajjoka, 2004

How to Pass Selection Tests, 3rd edition, Mike Bryon and Sanjay Modha, 2005

How to Pass Technical Selection Tests, 2nd edition, Mike Bryon and Sanjay Modha, 2005

How to Pass Verbal Reasoning Tests, 2nd edition, Harry Tolley and Ken Thomas, 2000

IQ and Psychometric Test Workbook, Philip Carter, 2005

Preparing Your Own CV: How to Improve Your Chances of Getting the Job You Want, 3rd edition, Rebecca Corfield, 2003

Readymade CVs: Sample CVs for Every Type of Job, 3rd edition, Lynn Williams, 2004

Readymade Job Search Letters: Every Type of Letter for Getting the Job You Want, 3rd edition, Lynn Williams, 2004

Successful Interview Skills, Rebecca Corfield, 1992

Test Your Own Aptitude, 3rd edition, Jim Barrett and Geoff Williams, 2003

The Times Book of IQ Tests: Book 1, Ken Russell and Philip Carter, 2001

The Times Book of IQ Tests: Book 2, Ken Russell and Philip Carter, 2002

The Times Book of IQ Tests: Book 3, Ken Russell and Philip Carter, 2003

The Times Book of IQ Tests: Book 4, Ken Russell and Philip Carter, 2004

The Ultimate Interview Book, Lynn Williams, 2005

CD ROMS

Psychometric Tests, Volume 1, The Times Testing Series, Editor Mike Bryon 2002

Test Your Aptitude, Volume 1, The Times Testing Series, Editor Mike Bryon, 2002

Test Your IQ, Volume 1, The Times Testing Series, Editor Mike Bryon, 2002

The above titles are available from all good bookshops. For further information, contact the publisher at the address below:

Kogan Page Limited
120 Pentonville Road
London N1 9JN
Tel: 020 7278 0433
Fax: 020 7837 6348
Website: www.kogan-page.co.uk

THE  TIMES

Published by Kogan Page Interactive, The Times Testing Series is an exciting new range of interactive CD ROMs that will provide invaluable practice tests for job applicants and for those seeking a brain-stretching challenge.

Each CD ROM features:

- hundreds of unique interactive questions
- instant scoring with feedback and analysis
- hours of practice and fun
- questions devised by top UK MENSA puzzle editors and test experts
- against-the-clock, real test conditions
- a program that allows users to create their own tests

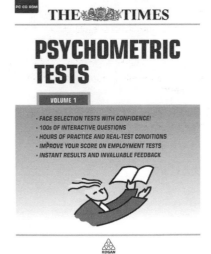

Psychometric Tests
Volume 1

Psychometric Tests Volume 1 provides essential practice for any job applicant who has to face a selection test.

With this CD ROM users will be able to:

- practise on tests based on those used by top employers
- learn how to tackle different types of questions
- experience real test conditions
- receive instant results and invaluable feedback

THE TIMES

Test Your IQ
Volume 1

This interactive CD ROM contains hundreds of questions just like those used in job selection IQ tests. *Test Your IQ* Volume 1 enables users to:

- practise for hours and achieve improved scores
- score against their friends
- develop their vocabulary and powers of logic
- practise on randomly selected tests every time

Test Your Aptitude
Volume 1

By working through the tests contained in this interactive CD ROM users will get a clear insight into what really makes them tick and the sort of job that would suit them best. *Test Your Aptitude* Volume 1 will reveal to users:

- what really motivates them
- which career best suits their personality
- their strengths and weaknesses
- how they will perform in selection tests

Available from all good bookshops, software outlets and the Kogan Page Web site. To obtain further information, please contact the publisher at the address below:

Kogan Page Ltd
120 Pentonville Road
London N1 9JN
Tel: 020 7278 0433
Fax: 020 7837 6348

www.kogan-page.co.uk